CONFIDENCE

CONFIDENCE
OF THE
HEART

David Schweidel

MILKWEED
EDITIONS

The characters and events in this book are fictitious. Any similarity to real persons, living or dead, is coincidental and not intended by the author.

Published in 1995 by Milkweed Editions
Printed in the United States of America
Book design by Will Powers. The text of this book is set in Plantin.

95 96 97 98 99   5 4 3 2 1

First Edition

Milkweed Editions is a not-for-profit publisher. We gratefully acknowledge support from the Dayton Hudson Foundation for Dayton's and Target Stores; Ecolab Foundation; General Mills Foundation; Honeywell Foundation; Jerome Foundation; John S. and James L. Knight Foundation; The McKnight Foundation; Andrew W. Mellon Foundation; Minnesota State Arts Board through an appropriation by the Minnesota State Legislature; Musser Fund; Challenge and Literature Programs of the National Endowment for the Arts; I. A. O'Shaughnessy Foundation; Piper Family Fund and the John and Beverly Rollwagen Fund of the Minneapolis Foundation; Piper Jaffray Companies, Inc.; The St. Paul Companies, Inc.; Star Tribune / Cowles Media Foundation; Surdna Foundation; James R. Thorpe Foundation; Unity Avenue Foundation; Lila Wallace-Reader's Digest Literary Publishers Marketing Development Program, funded through a grant to the Council of Literary Magazines and Presses; and generous individuals.

Library of Congress Cataloging-in-Publication Data

Schweidel, David.
    Confidence of the heart / David Schweidel.
        p.   cm.
    ISBN 1-57131-004-5
    I. Title
PS3569.C56815C66   1995   94–33644
813´.54–dc20   CIP

This book is printed on acid-free paper.

*With thanks to my mother, Jean; my sisters
and brothers, Susan, Judy, Kim, Billy,
and their families; poets David Rivard, Tony
Hoagland, and George Shelton; fiction writers
Robert Boswell and Antonya Nelson;
rock'n'roller Mark Russell; Kim Witherspoon;
Emilie Buchwald; Rudolfo Anaya; the Newell
family; the Lozano family; Betty Sasaki; and
most especially Linda Steele.*

IN MEMORY OF THE COLONEL

The domination of a large group of powerless people has long since ceased being totalitarianism's most typical feature. Nowadays, what is typical is the domination of one part of ourselves by another part of ourselves. It's as if the regime had an outpost inside every citizen.

VACLAV HAVEL

The most feared enemy is within oneself in the confidence of the heart.

GABRIEL GARCÍA MÁRQUEZ

CONFIDENCE
OF THE
HEART

I

A CERTAIN SAFE DISTANCE

And what if after so much history
we succumb not to eternity
but to these simple things, like being
at home, or starting to brood.

CESAR VALLEJO

Evidently, the change machine was broken. According to the cranky attorney hovering over my cubicle, it had devoured her five-dollar bill. I kept typing just long enough to communicate that the change machine was not my responsibility and then hustled into the support-staff lounge to fix it.

As soon as the lights went out, I realized that I was the target of a plot. Someone giggled in the darkness. A dim glow at the far end of the lounge gradually revealed a cake crammed with flickering candles being carried toward me by a procession of shadowy figures. I'll never forget the heat rising from those candles. Thirty candles throw a lot of heat. When I leaned forward to blow them out, the burning on my cheeks made me pull back. I caught sight of my reflection in the sepia-tinted window superimposed over the view of the adjacent high-rise. It occurred to me that I should have taken the night off even if I had nothing special to do.

Though I appreciated the efforts of the other word processors, my effusive thanks rang false. I couldn't stop glancing at the reflection in the window. Every detail of my circumstances began to seem pathetic: the slice of blue cake on a plastic plate, the Styrofoam cup of pink champagne. The proofreader gave me a beautiful hardcover edition of *The Selected Poems of Rainer Maria Rilke,* but I felt uncomfortable accepting such a substantial gift.

Our party ended after less than five minutes when the cranky attorney reappeared. "Glad to help with your little surprise," she said, "but now I really do need to get home. Could anyone who isn't too busy run fetch me a cab voucher?"

No one answered. The condescending catch in the attorney's voice offended us.

"No problem," I finally said.

I must have kept my sarcasm to myself, because the proofreader called me the saint of the swing shift when she walked me to the elevator a short while later.

"I could write a whole book about how that cow demanded a cab voucher," she said. "*Anyone who isn't too busy. Run fetch.* Only a saint could be so polite."

"I thought I was kind of subversive," I said, stepping into the elevator.

"Feel like a birthday cappuccino?" the proofreader said. "I'll grab my purse and leave that last set of interrogatories for the day shift."

"I wish I could," I said.

"What about a birthday scotch? You need to get out more. Heard from Lorna lately?"

The elevator doors slid shut, sparing me the need to respond. Lorna had been a receptionist at the law firm before she moved to New York to pursue her painting and modeling career. Our unlikely liaison had astonished everyone on the twenty-ninth floor. "Are you still hung up on Lorna?" was what the proofreader had wanted to ask. Afraid to consider the answer, I suddenly noticed the stillness of the elevator. It wasn't going anywhere.

"Boy, boy, boy," I muttered. Gazing up at the mirrored ceiling, I saw myself slumped in a corner, alone and looking lost. I pressed the button for the lobby. The elevator, as usual, started down, but nothing seemed usual anymore.

At the Embarcadero BART station, I stood a safe step back from the edge of the platform. I couldn't help imagining an accidental bump from behind, my clumsy plunge to the tracks, the prolonged instant of panic as I braced for impact. When the train surged into the station, I reached between the buttons of my plain white shirt and touched the pink cross my father left me; then I boarded the train and barricaded myself behind my briefcase.

No one talked. An old man in a Giants baseball cap snoozed with his mouth open. A woman in a trench coat watched people's reflections in the dark windows. BART, I decided, had been designed to discourage human contact.

The woman in the trench coat stared straight at me, moving her lips slowly. I had the feeling she was reading my mind. I opened my briefcase and took out the Rilke book. There was something strange about the woman, stranger than her trench coat, pink socks, and green bowling shoes, stranger than her hair dyed the color of corn. She had no eyebrows. None. Just two crooked lines drawn in thick with what appeared to be yellow crayon.

When she started to sing, I concentrated on the book. A telltale birthday bow still clung to it. I put the bow back in my briefcase with my newspaper and used lunch bag.

"Everything Is Beautiful," she sang, first to herself and then to the whole car. She stopped when the train stopped at 16th Street, went on when the train went on. I tried to concentrate on a poem, but her thin, nasal voice commanded my attention.

She sang into her fist as if it were a microphone. She staggered in my direction and held her fist up to my face. Sweat beaded her upper lip. Her black thumbnail was bitten past the quick. I sat there like a rock until she moved on to the old man in the Giants cap, who had the grace to croak out a few notes. She opened her fist and caressed his wrinkled cheek with the palm of her hand.

I got off then, at 24th and Mission, trudged up the escalator (out of service since Christmas), and refused a flyer from the Pentecostal preacher. The smell of McDonald's mingled with cumin, cilantro, and roast pork. I plodded down Mission as I always did, past the *taquerías* and the lesbian coffee shop. Just another night, I told myself, crossing Army Street in front of a metallic green Impala, chopped low, with the Virgin of Guadalupe stenciled on the hood.

Climbing the stairs to my apartment, scanning the dreary phone bill and library bulletin that had arrived in the mail, I felt the full, inelegant weight of my life. The slap of quick footsteps sounded behind me. Before I could turn around, someone wrapped me in a bear hug and squeezed.

"*Viva la revolución!*" a demented voice hissed in my ear.

I threw my head back but failed to connect. Then I kicked backward and caught all shin. The grip weakened. I scrambled up to the landing and spun around, crouching to protect myself.

I should have known it would be Spoon at the bottom of the stairs. Who but my best friend would have exerted so much energy on my account? I patted my father's cross in relief.

"Aren't you glad to see me?" Spoon said. He looked like a derelict down there, hopping on one leg and rubbing the other, his purple serape flapping wildly. "I bribed half the airport guys in Guatemala to get here on time."

"You shouldn't have," I said.

"You don't understand. I've come to save you." He turned on the tape recorder strapped across his serape like a bandito's cartridge belt and spoke into the microphone. "We're outside the home of Armando Santiesteban, internationally famous *bon vivant*, on the historic occasion of his thirtieth birthday. Armando, how does it feel to cross the threshold into middle age? Is there life after thirty—or what?"

"No comment," I said, intending to resist, but even my resistance played into his game.

He flashed a triumphant grin, collected his duffel bag and my briefcase, and valiantly hobbled up the stairs. I didn't offer to help, but he pretended I did.

"No, no, no," he said. "Allow me."

Spoon and I had met at the University of California, Berkeley. By what logic the dormitory masters assigned us to the same room, we never guessed. Most of the other freshmen seemed matched by size. Spoon was six-foot-six and weighed a hundred fifty-nine pounds. No one was his size.

Our sophomore year we shared an apartment with my high-school sweetheart, Betsy Fairbanks. When Betsy and I got married, Spoon sponsored our honeymoon. After that he dropped out for a while. The police arrested him for picketing with the United Farm Workers. He was pyramid-hopping in the

Yucatan when I graduated with high honors and received a scholarship to Harvard Law School.

Two years later, just before the end of my summer internship with a large Boston law firm, I suffered a kind of breakdown, a severe loss of will. I flew home to Reedley, California, and tormented my parents for a week, and then, instead of returning to law school and marriage, I moved into a cheap hotel in the Mission District of San Francisco. I called my wife every night—from a pay phone, collect. She always accepted the charges. She did her best to cushion my fall. But I wanted to hit bottom. I wanted to live like the failure I felt myself to be.

Disaster attracts disaster, I discovered after less than a month. My father smashed his pickup truck into a utility pole and died on the way to the hospital. He was forty-nine years old. My wife stayed with me after the funeral—until I managed to convince her that love does not conquer all. She scrubbed my dank walls with ammonia, stockpiled plenty of canned soup and broccoli, and kissed me tenderly good-bye.

After that I was free to make the worst of things. For more than a year, I slept and ate and collected welfare. I put on fifty pounds. My mother tried to haul me back to Reedley, but I was too heavy.

I can't explain my determination to suffer. One night Spoon knocked on my door, but I wouldn't answer. He was a hotshot graduate student by then, eager to commiserate. "Open up," he said. "This is kid stuff." I remember him shouting my name, pounding and pounding, while I stood on my side of the door, waiting for it to splinter.

Forgive me for dwelling on this personal debacle. Maybe *kid stuff* was a fair diagnosis. There are diseases mild in childhood that can kill an adult.

Eventually, my wife filed for divorce. The arrival of the official decree provided a bottom to push off against. I started working for a temporary agency in the financial district. A law firm offered me a permanent job. After a long stretch of indifference, I lucked into a decent apartment and lost some weight.

Spoon, by this time, had done fieldwork in Guatemala and

begun writing his dissertation. When his father suffered his first heart attack, Spoon came to my apartment, and the odd chemistry of consolation reconnected us somehow. In spite of our conflicting schedules, we started doing things together again, playing racquetball, seeing movies. He even dragged me along on a few of his dates.

Then a woman at work, Lorna, actually took an interest in me. Spoon dismissed her as a typical artist/receptionist/feminist/exhibitionist, but I spent more and more time with her, and less with him, until she moved to New York. Shortly afterwards, Spoon went back to Guatemala to fine-tune his dissertation and the next thing I knew I was being attacked by a maniac right outside my apartment.

Spoon's first order of business was to inspect my head for gray hair. I didn't have any. He untucked my shirt and thumped my ample belly.

"Definite reduction of quiver," he said.

"Too kind," I said.

"You okay?" he said, unpacking a bottle of *Gusano Rojo* and a tin cup. "I've got good news. My dissertation has been approved."

"Great," I said.

"University of Texas Press may publish it."

"That's really great," I said.

"*And!*" he said. He brought the kitchen stool into the middle of the room and vaulted onto it. "*And*, a small but prestigious Connecticut college has offered me a tenure-track job. Assistant professor of anthropology."

I sank to my knees and salaamed. I'm not that demonstrative most of the time, but a little of Spoon's flamboyance must have rubbed off.

"*And!*" he said again.

"There's more?"

"I'm getting married," he said.

I backed into the corner on my knees. My kneecaps throbbed. Bent low, I spotted dust balls under the bookshelf where the vacuum wouldn't reach. A broom wouldn't reach there either. Maybe a damp paper towel poked in with a wire hanger...I pondered this housecleaning problem until Spoon's feet intervened.

The rainbow soles of his enormous flip-flops seemed indecently cheerful.

"I'm really happy for you," I finally managed to say.

He held his right arm behind his back as if I were twisting it. "Since you insist, I'll tell you about her. She's beautiful. She's Guatemalan. María Magdalena de Montenegro Schultz. How's that for a moniker?"

I lapsed into the fetal position.

"What gives?" he said. He looked like Christ up there. Despite his scruffy beard and ratty red ponytail, he looked like Christ the night of the Last Supper: concerned about poor Judas, but still ecstatic at his own prospects.

"I don't know," I said. I wanted to jump up and shake his hand, but I couldn't. "Work was strange tonight. The change machine broke. Or maybe it didn't. But the elevator got stuck. Or else I pressed the wrong button. All I know is I felt stuck. I'm thirty and I'm stuck." I lay on the floor and looked up at Spoon.

"Come to Guatemala and be my best man," he said.

"I'm too fat," I said. "I look bad in a tux."

"I'm asking you to be my best man," he said. "All expenses paid. We leave day after tomorrow."

A handful of brightly colored Guatemalan bills fluttered to the floor around me.

"That's generous," I said. "But I doubt the law firm would let me off on such short notice."

"You complain about being stuck, but you love it," Spoon said. "It's time to destroy the past."

"Sounds drastic," I said.

"I have in mind a simple ceremony. We say good-bye to our old lives and welcome the new."

"I'll just watch," I said.

He pulled a crumpled grocery bag out of his duffel. "People become so attached to certain objects, certain memories, they don't know how to let go." He held the bag at arm's length, as if it were the prized head of a noble enemy. "They're all in here," he said. "All my old girlfriends."

"How nice for you," I said.

"A ritual sacrifice," he said. "For Magdalena. We'll sacrifice them to the god of fire."

It was cool out on the balcony. The slice of white moon over Sutro Tower paled in thickening fog. There are two basic ways to build a barbecue fire, the Santiesteban method, which I learned from my mother and my mother learned from Dear Abby, and the pyromaniac method, preferred by Spoon and my father and Mrs. O'Leary's cow. I put a paper towel at the bottom of the hibachi, stacked the charcoal into a pyramid, squeezed on a little lighter fluid, gave it time to soak in, and then, all risk avoided, lit a corner of the paper towel and watched the fire gradually spread. Spoon shuffled his photographs like a cardsharp stacking a deck and dealt me the top photograph.

"Irene Pouspourika," he said. "My eighth birthday. The godforsaken isle of Crete." A dark-haired girl with a strong Greek nose was feeding Spoon a cupcake while a smaller girl clung to his back.

"Is that your little sister?" I asked.

"That was her," he said. "That was Mary Alice."

"God," I said. "She looked just like you."

"Yeah," he said. "We called her the Sherpa because she loved to climb on things, me in particular. She died five months after this was taken." He touched her face with his finger before dropping the photograph into the fire. It curled as it burned.

The second photograph came from Paraguay, the courtyard of an old Spanish-style hacienda with a broom and a woman's plump arms just visible in the lower right-hand corner.

"The only trace of Josefina left," Spoon said.

"I'm not sure I want to hear this story again."

"She was really sweet. I used to do my homework in the laundry room while she ironed. She'd sing these amazing ballads. Love and death mixed up together. The smell of starch and bleach. Her teeth were really crooked, but I liked her breath."

"I can't believe you had sex when you were thirteen," I said.

When the phone rang a few minutes later, Spoon was conjuring up his high school *novia* from Santiago, Chile. "If that's

Lorna," he said, "tell her to bug off. Tell her a lifetime vow of silence wouldn't be long enough."

It was my mother. "I hope you're not all alone on your birthday," she said, but she sounded disappointed when I told her that Spoon was visiting. The truth is that my mother loves the *pobrecito* routine. She wants me to be happy, but only with her help.

"Anything wrong?" I said. I always hear so much grief in my mother's voice over the phone.

"No, no, dear," she said. "I'm the happiest woman in the world. It's just that the Maverick's passed on."

Spoon opened my mail, read my phone bill, yanked Lorna's abstract oil painting off its hook. Meanwhile, my mother's car had broken down, the new manager at the coffee shop was not well bred, but my brother had made salutatorian and the teachers were saying the same wonderful things about him they'd said about me.

Spoon pulled down the snapshots taped above my bed. Paint chips stuck to the tape.

I told my mother that Spoon was getting married. "There's a slight possibility I may go to Guatemala this weekend."

"Slight possibility?" Spoon said in disgust.

"It's dangerous down that way," my mother said. "Besides, they need you at work. And the expense."

"Thanks for the encouragement," I said.

"I just want you to be safe," she said. "Give Spoon a hug for me. Tons of love to you both."

Spoon dumped a whole shelf of law books on the floor as I hung up. "Your turn to burn," he said, gesturing at the room as if nothing in it should be spared the torch.

"I'm not the one whose life is changing," I said.

"That's because you hold on to it so tight." He waved the snapshots in my face. "How do you expect to get laid with a picture of your ex-wife over your bed?"

"I don't expect to get laid."

"You need another drink. Too much moderation is a dangerous thing."

"How would you know?"

"Just do me a favor," he said. "Burn one picture, one post-card, one ticket stub."

I went into the walk-in closet and sat down in front of the re-cessed chest of drawers. I felt comfortable on the closet floor, even with Spoon looming over me. I breathed easy for the first time that day. Of course I couldn't destroy anything important. Finally, I pulled out a stack of canceled checks.

"Don't go overboard," Spoon said.

True to the pyromaniac school, he flooded the gray coals with lighter fluid and tossed on a match. The flames leaped higher than the balcony railing.

I read each check before I burned it. Spoon insisted. It was a peculiar form of oral history: PG&E, Safeway, my wife. The ef-fect was out of proportion, unsettling and invigorating at the same time. The fog dropped down low, Spoon poured a modest shot, and—for his sake—I drank it. Then he handed me the snapshot of my wife with her new husband and the deaf Dalmatian she and I had once rescued from the Boston pound. The fog made me shiver. I buttoned my corduroy coat.

"Burn it," Spoon said. "Get her out of your system."

"It wouldn't make any difference," I said.

"Of course not," he said. "So what's stopping you?"

"I like this picture," I said. "I like having it."

"That's the difference," he said. "You wouldn't have it any-more."

I lowered the snapshot close to the fire, considered letting it go, and then slipped it into my pocket.

Spoon paced the balcony. "You're such a sentimentalist," he said. He pulled out my other snapshot, which showed him and a medical anthropology student named Hester, along with Lorna and me, posed at a Halloween party as the Four Mousketeers, complete with capes, Mickey Mouse hats, and plastic swords. Lorna was avidly licking the tip of her sword. "At least burn this one," Spoon said. "It might prove incrimi-nating. Magdalena thinks I haven't dated much."

A stiff breeze sent a popsicle wrapper swirling upwards. The snapshot of Lorna flew out of Spoon's hand and skittered up the street. Our fire had died down, but the whitish coals still glowed red at the edges.

"Let's go in," I said.

"Let's go out," he said. "I've arranged a little entertainment for your benefit."

"You've arranged entertainment? You just flew into town."

"Connections," he said. "Besides, I didn't really arrange it. I just got permission to horn in."

"It's late," I said. "I'm beat."

"The night is prepubescent. You need to sacrifice a few more things. Lorna's jive-ass joke of a painting, for instance."

"It may be a collector's item some day."

"Not if we burn it."

He planted his elbow on the balcony railing. I did the same. Whenever we drank more than three shots of mescal, we ended up arm wrestling.

"Give up your past and journey out into the world," he said. The tendon along his forearm throbbed.

"I prefer to keep a certain safe distance." I threw my weight away from the street and toward my apartment.

"I noticed a collect call from New York on your phone bill," he said.

"Lorna needed her tax forms."

"Perfect," he grunted. "Not only does she use you, she uses you *collect*."

My arm dipped an inch toward the street. I concentrated on my breathing.

"You can't stay on the balcony forever." Spoon pressed his advantage. "No man is a balcony unto himself."

My arm collapsed. My whole body sagged. If losing builds character, I had a major edifice under construction.

"Which law book do you hate the most?" Spoon called, ducking inside to throw a few burnables into my briefcase. "How about *Civil Procedure*?" He ripped out a handful of pages and flung them toward the ceiling. They floated to the floor, the formerly tidy floor, among the Guatemalan bills that resembled play money, his jackknifed duffel, my vanquished law books.

"You should thank me for this," he said. "I'm doing you a favor."

I pointed to the hibachi. "What about the fire?"

"They've got their own fire," he said.

"They?" I asked, but he was already out the door.

And so it came to pass that on the night of my thirtieth birthday, I marched down Coleridge Street with an abstract painting balanced on my head. Spoon led the way to the vacant lot behind Mona's House of Beauty, where a cowboy and a Mayan Indian were tending a fire fueled by railroad ties and lumberyard scraps. Between the fire and the heap of wood, a wobbly card table held a bucket, a black candle, and a few objects less recognizable.

The men accepted our intrusion without comment. We stared at the fire, absorbed its heat, listened to the flames lap and crackle. No one spoke. There was enough light from the fire and the corner streetlights to illuminate the mural of Mona Lisa in curlers on the back wall of the beauty parlor.

"Did a guy named Ricardo from the Guatemalan Action Network mention we'd be dropping by?" Spoon asked.

"That *cabrón* owes me twenty bucks," the cowboy said, grimacing as if to show off his blackened front tooth.

Unfazed, Spoon poured a shot of mescal into his tin cup and passed it to the Mayan, who crossed himself with the cup and swallowed hard. If you live in the Mission long enough, you develop an instinct for who's legal and who's not. The Mayan was definitely legal. I could tell from his faded leather jacket, his healthy paunch, and the casual way he checked his watch, a flashy Rolex much too massive for his thin wrist.

"I'm Patrick McGuffin," Spoon said, insisting on full introductions and hearty American handshakes. "I'm getting married in Guatemala next week. Listen, you mind if we borrow your fire?" He jerked his thumb at Lorna's painting. "We want to burn that monster. Armando's last girlfriend did it. You know what she put him through? Last fall she convinced him to take her to opening night of the opera. Now I ask you, is this an opera buff? No, but he was in love. He rented a tux. He slapped on the English Leather, adjusted his cummerbund, and then, after he'd gotten all ready to go pick her up, she called him from the airport and said she was moving to New York. From the *airport!* The opera tickets alone cost a hundred bucks!"

What Spoon and I were doing must have seemed like a silly game to these men, but they paid us the respect of saying nothing, even when Spoon grabbed the painting from me and held it out to his side, matador style.

"Kick it in," he said. The painting—overlapping bands of purple, black, blue, and yellow—resembled a deep bruise, but I had nothing against it. "Work up some rage." He thrust the painting forward like a cape. "Say something. Talk about her. What did she do that you hate?"

"Nothing. She gave me the painting because my walls were bare. She disapproved of bare walls."

"You can do better than that," Spoon said.

I felt terribly self-conscious. Claude, the freckled cowboy with the black tooth, cracked his knuckles. Sonny Tzoc, the paunchy Mayan, looked on with the sober composure of a judge. I dabbed my face with a handkerchief. To discuss my private life in front of strangers put me into a sweat.

"You like kiss?" Sonny said.

I covered my mouth in surprise. His question defied interpretation—until he brought out a bag of chocolate kisses and gently jiggled one into my hand. Rarely have I appreciated a sweet so much. His eyes, which had seemed so stern a moment before, now seemed sympathetic.

"I was alone for a long time," I said. "I mean, I was married for three and a half years, and after that I mostly kept to myself. The first woman to take an interest in me, the first woman since my wife, was the woman who painted that picture. I don't know why she liked me."

"You were the ethnic type," Spoon said.

"I think I was kind of a charity case." I directed my confession to Sonny, who bobbed his head as I spoke. "Our first date she invited me to a party where everyone stripped naked and painted each other with finger paint. I pretended it was no big deal, but . . . I don't know. The point is—my walls *were* bare."

"Are you gonna kick that sucker in?" Claude said. "I'll do her if you want."

"No," Spoon said. "Let him do her."

"That frame's worth something," Claude said. "I wouldn't mind that frame."

I scraped my foot back and forth like a bull about to charge. For the first time I seriously envisioned putting my gray Hush Puppy loafer through Lorna's canvas. It didn't seem quite so far-fetched anymore.

While I deliberated, a second Mayan slunk up among us, cradling a delicate object wrapped in a baby blanket. This Mayan did not look legal. He was too twitchy in his off-brand designer jeans. Sonny offered him a kiss and Spoon offered him a shot, but he just glared at both of them and unwrapped the object in the blanket, a devilish effigy stuffed with straw, more like a scarecrow than anything else, a miniature scarecrow complete with sombrero, cigar, and black wooden mask.

"Please forgive my brother's preoccupation," Sonny said. "His wife is very sick."

"I'm sorry," Spoon said. "Do you mind if I ask a question? Did your brother make that *imagen* himself?"

"Ignacio brought the *imagen* from his village. His village is where the *imagen* belongs."

Ignacio lit the black candle and placed the *imagen* beside it on the card table. Claude took a bowl-shaped piece of gourd and floated it on top of the water in the bucket. I was confused. I didn't realize Claude was constructing a musical instrument. When he struck the gourd with a stick wrapped in corn husks, it made a deep, liquid, penetrating sound: *bome, bome, bome*.

Spoon, pretending to stretch, switched on his tape recorder. I frowned at him, but he just grinned.

"That's rude," I whispered.

"It's anthropology," he said.

Sonny picked up a wooden flute, which he played one-handed—short, sharp notes like the cry of a frightened bird—while Claude beat the drum and Ignacio unzipped his black boots. The flames cast quicksilver shapes in the mind's eye. Ignacio balanced on his right foot and then his left; he bent low and danced between the *imagen* and the fire. His movements possessed an impressive weight, as if the earth's gravity pulled more strongly on his slight body. He seemed to be trying to shed a heavy burden. I felt uncomfortable just watching. The *imagen* wasn't the only one who belonged elsewhere.

"I'm going home," I whispered to Spoon.

"Not yet," Spoon said.

We must have distracted Ignacio, because all of a sudden he pounced in front of us and shouted in a language I'd never heard before. There was no mistaking his meaning, though.

I would have left immediately, but Spoon kicked off his flip-flops and flexed his knees. "Our apologies," he said. "We intend no disrespect. In fact, it would be our honor to participate in your ceremony. May I dance?"

Ignacio stared at Spoon with an expression wavering between amazement and disgust while Sonny translated. I don't know why they let us stay, but curiosity may have been a factor, the urge to see what the redhead in the purple serape would do next.

Claude laid down the same steady drumbeat as before, but Sonny held back on the flute, as if he didn't quite trust Spoon. Gradually, though, the tension of the music built. Shoulders thrust forward, head raised high, Spoon shuffled his feet slowly, like a soft-shoe artist. Although his dancing lacked the urgency of Ignacio's, it was no joke. He moved with conviction, concentrating on every step. The song ended all of a sudden when everyone simply stopped.

Ignacio pointed a crooked finger at me. I noticed his clunky Rolex, identical to Sonny's, glinting in the light of the fire.

"I don't dance," I said.

"Do whatever you want," Sonny said.

"This guy is good," Spoon said. "He used to give speeches to the Rotary Club."

I thought of the woman on the BART train, her clenched fist in my face. I'd already passed up one chance to perform that night. All I wanted was to be back on my balcony, a safe distance from the unpredictable demands of the world. If I had begun to imagine how drastically those demands would increase during the next week, I would have rushed home and locked myself in the closet, but instead I opened my briefcase and found the book I'd hidden behind on the train.

"Can I read you a poem?" I asked. "There's one in here that I keep taped to my cubicle at work. It's about an old statue, so old the head got knocked off years ago, but even just the body seems to see deep into you."

My voice was shaky as I recited the poem, but everyone listened. Sonny clasped his hands together as if I were praying.

"That's it," I said when I finished. "That's the whole poem."

Spoon grinned. Ignacio heaped two armloads of wood onto the fire, pyromaniac style. Sonny and Claude sat cross-legged in the shadows and made the music of dreams—bad dreams, a nightmarish chase through the jungle. The flute leaped from note to piercing note. The water drum beat like a troubled heart.

Ignacio held the black candle up to the *imagen* and lit the cigar. I wondered what the *imagen* meant to him, how it compared to the old statue in Rilke's poem. Black wax dripped on Ignacio's hand and he let it solidify.

"*Maximón*," he said. He might have been waking a dreaming friend. "*Maximón.*"

He danced the *imagen* and the candle in front of us like two puppets. He began to chant in a hypnotic undertone words I couldn't understand.

The random notes of the flute began to seem less random after awhile. I thought I heard a pattern of repetition and variation, an emotional progression from fright to resolve. Ignacio stood more and more upright as he danced, as if his spirits were lightening.

Meanwhile, Spoon pulled the last few photographs from his bag of girlfriends. Hester, Carmen, Gita, Ruth—I knew them by first name only.

Ignacio lowered his voice as he edged closer to the flames. When he finally stopped, arched over the flames like a *banderillero* over a bull, the drums and the flute played on.

He snuffed the black candle out against his forehead and flung it behind him. Then, as carefully as a mother would lay a baby in the cradle, he lay the *imagen* on the fire. His hands seemed to linger in the flames. His gaunt face glistened. "You must change your life," Spoon whispered, echoing the poem I'd recited. He planted Lorna's painting right beside me.

Even abrupt changes occur extraordinarily slowly. The temperature rises degree by degree before ice turns to water, water to steam. I felt as though something inside me had been heating up for ages.

I turned and kicked Lorna's painting, but not hard enough, or else Spoon lost his grip, because my Hush Puppy bounced off the canvas. I kicked again, and the canvas ripped, flapping loose like a broken wing.

The music must have ended at about that time. Sonny and Claude started lobbing firecrackers into the fire, hammerheads and black cats that flashed as they popped. Ignacio inhaled the smoke as if it were pure oxygen.

I kicked Lorna's painting again. Spoon kicked it, Claude kicked it, and then Spoon cut out the scraps of canvas with his Swiss army knife.

Despite Ignacio's lack of fire-building technique, there was an intricate structure at the heart of the fire, a glowing red chamber. I shoved the wadded canvas in there, along with *Civil Procedure*, which burned with the stench of tar.

When Ignacio finally bent in half with coughing, Sonny and Claude quickly pulled his black T-shirt over his head. Sonny signed the cross and whispered what must have been a prayer.

I dusted off my briefcase. I was ready to leave. Spoon picked up the stub of the black candle, sniffed it, and tossed it away. He reminded me of a kid at Christmas who'd opened all his presents but still expected more: where's the ten-speed? the Shetland pony? A siren sounded from the direction of Noe Valley. Spoon latched onto Lorna's picture frame and bounded toward me.

"Guatemala," he said with his irrefutable grin. He held the frame suspended above my head like a halo.

"I still have misgivings," I said.

"No, you have *reservations*," he said, slowly lowering the frame around me until it rested on the ground. "Step out of the frame."

"Why?"

"You are *so close* to crossing a threshold. Just one more step."
A second siren started up somewhere on Portrero Hill.
Several neighborhood dogs joined in.

"Guatemala," Spoon said again. "You never regret the things
you do — only the things you don't do." He unfolded the
longest blade on his Swiss army knife and sawed off his ponytail. "See how easy it is?" He chucked the hair into the fire.

"Gestures are great," I said. "But they have to be genuine.
They don't mean anything if they're not genuine."

"That's where you're wrong," he said. "The gesture *becomes*
the feeling. That's the secret of ritual."

He draped his serape over one side of the frame like a gentleman about to escort a lady across a puddle. He even offered his
hand while the wail of converging sirens rose from the hollow in
the pit of my stomach to the knot at the top of my throat.

"I'll cross your cosmic threshold, but that doesn't mean I'll
go to Guatemala," I said, stepping out of the frame as the first of
two fire trucks and three police cars arrived at our vacant lot.

Before Spoon had a chance to argue, we were handcuffed
and on our way to jail.

The Mission Station gave me a headache. The fluorescent lights
hurt my eyes and the twangy country music operated on my
nerves like a dental drill. While Spoon harassed the desk
sergeant, I fretted over the possibility of spending the night in a
cell. *Guilt by association* was the phrase that looped through my
mind, even though the arresting officer had advised us not to
worry. "Procedure, gentlemen," he'd said, uncuffing us at the
station and leaving us unguarded next to the vending machines.
The assumption seemed to be that we wouldn't dare try to escape without our driver's licenses.

After Spoon bought a round of sodas and Sonny Tzoc told a
funny story about his job as an elementary school janitor, my
mood improved. The late hour and the sterile surroundings un-
accountably encouraged conversation.

"Are you really getting married in Guatemala next week?"
Sonny asked Spoon.

"Unless I wise up," Spoon said.

"My oldest brother still lives in Guatemala," Sonny said. "I haven't heard from him in a year."

"I got married in Guatemala," Claude said. "Worst mistake of my youth."

Spoon frowned. "Getting married or getting married in Guatemala?"

"Same difference," Claude said.

"What was your impression of Guatemala?" I asked.

"It's like anyplace else—it's a foreign country."

The arresting officer interrupted us. "Which one of you is Juan Mendoza?" he said.

"He is," Sonny said, indicating Ignacio.

"Well then, let me direct my questions to him." The officer spoke in a tone of polite contempt it must have taken years to master.

"Do we have a problem here?" Spoon said.

"I certainly hope not." The officer pointed to Ignacio's bony wrist. "Heck of a watch. Mind if I try it on?"

Ignacio, after a nudge from Sonny, slipped off the Rolex.

"My partner's birthday's coming up and it's so hard to find the right gift," the officer said. "How much does a watch like this cost, if I may ask?"

"Only around fifty bucks," Sonny said. He pronounced bucks like *box*, and the officer repeated the mispronunciation.

"Fifty box. Amazing."

"My neighbor buys them in Hong Kong. He says it's one lifetime deal." Sonny pushed up the sleeve of his leather jacket to reveal his own gold watch.

The officer heaved his sagging chest in my direction.

"I wear a Timex from Sears," I said in faultless, unaccented English. I have to admit I wanted to distinguish myself from Sonny and Ignacio.

"I don't believe we're required to show you our watches," Spoon said.

I poked him in the ribs. *Take it easy*, I signaled with my hands. It didn't do any good, though. Once it was established that Juan Mendoza's driver's license was bogus, Spoon went into his champion-of-the-downtrodden act, demanding that everyone be allowed to go home.

"Careful, lad," the world-weary officer said, an edge of threat in his voice.

I wedged myself between Spoon and the officer, lowered my shoulder into Spoon's chest, and drove him back a step.

"It's common-sense time," I said.

"They'll nail our buddy," Spoon said. "Besides, why should I listen to you? I mean, if it was my best man talking, I might listen, but you—"

The officer was already escorting Ignacio to an interrogation room, not holding him exactly but steadying him the way you'd steady a jumpy colt. Spoon suddenly charged after them. I caught him by a corner of his serape.

"Wait!" I said, but he barely slowed down. "Okay, okay. I'll go to Guatemala. I'll be your best man. Just drop this now."

He let me drag him to a stop. "You'll come to Guatemala and be my best man?" he said. "On your father's cross?"

"If you behave," I said.

Ignacio never needed our help. Once the police determined that there were no warrants for his arrest, they released him. They didn't seem to care whether he was legal or not. The clerk who returned our driver's licenses even told Ignacio where to find a better fake ID.

Saying good-bye outside the station, Spoon took Sonny's address and asked if there was anything we could do for him in Guatemala.

"Oh, no," Sonny said. "My brother's region is very isolated."

"We'll be pretty busy," Spoon said. "But hell, we may need an excuse to dodge the wedding blitz."

Sonny tapped me on the shoulder. "You. Would you take something to my brother?"

"We'll do our best," Spoon said.

"I want *him*," Sonny said to Spoon. He tapped me on the shoulder again. "I want you."

"Sure," I said, already imagining the life sentence I'd probably serve for smuggling contraband chocolate kisses. "We'll stop by your house tomorrow."

"I appreciate," Sonny said.

As Spoon and I headed down Valencia Street, we overheard Claude mutter behind us, "Those boys got no idea what they're getting into."

The fog had lifted. The city at dawn was blessedly quiet. Spoon and I walked without talking for a minute.

"I haven't slept with Magdalena yet," Spoon eventually said. "Can you imagine? I'm giving up every other woman in the world, at least in theory."

"I'm sure she's worth it," I said.

"In a lot of ways, she's ideal," he said. "Most rich Guatemalans have this formal, stick-up-the-ass quality, but not Magdalena, although she's reserved. You get the feeling she's hiding something special and you have to seek it out. What I'm afraid of is that there's nothing special there, just the act of hiding itself. Know what I mean?"

I didn't know what he meant, but I nodded. The prospect of marriage reduced me to the least fatuous platitude I could think of. "Doubts before the wedding are traditional."

Spoon kicked a crumpled beer can off the sidewalk. "On the flight from Guatemala, I dreamed I was Lou Gehrig. Pride of the Yankees. Remember the scene in the movie when Lou is dying of Lou Gehrig's disease—your number's definitely up when you catch your own disease—and it's Lou Gehrig Day at Yankee Stadium, and Lou addresses the fans? 'Today-ay-ay. I-I. Am the happiest-appiest. Man-an-an. In the world-orld-rld.' Or does he say 'luckiest'? Anyway, there I was, addressing the fans, my voice reverberating through the stadium, and I didn't know if I was really happy, or really dying inside, or what."

I'd never seen Valencia Street at sunrise before. The dawn light cast even the sleaziest bars and boarded-up storefronts in a redemptive glow. I had no wisdom to offer Spoon. My life had accelerated beyond recognition. As we walked along together, the air shimmering like handblown glass, I decided to let the world around us convince Spoon of his luck. And me of mine.

II

CRUDITY VERSUS PRUDITY

Just the facts, ma'am.
JOE FRIDAY

Well, I thought I could hold my peace but I can't.

Here's the deal. Not long after our trip to Guatemala, Armando sent me a thick manuscript, which I promptly buried in the nether regions of my file cabinet. Now, due to circumstances beyond my control, I'm entombed in my office in the basement of the Study of Man building, typing my old friend's magnum opus on my laptop.

Put yourself in my place for a minute. Imagine the muffled click of the keys, the occasional pseudo-innocuous beep. Your chest tightens. Your mouth goes dry. Because, worst of all, you're typing lies. No, *lies* is too strong a word. *Mejor dicho,* half lies. Quarter lies. Agonizingly incomplete versions of the truth.

Incomplete, but not brief. Armando buries the truth under a mountain of details. Okay, I exaggerate. A pile of details. But a massive pile.

How massive? Well, instead of simply mentioning that we ran errands on Friday and drove south on Saturday, Armando throws in the recipe for the McGuffin Prairie Oyster I prepared for breakfast (Worcestershire sauce, Tabasco, brown sugar, and raw egg), the brand of gum my dissertation director chewed when we met with her in Berkeley (Double Bubble), the title of the management stooge who granted Armando's time-off request (Human Resources Coordinator), the source of the checks I deposited at the bank (trust fund), the colors of my hair stylist's hair (purple and gold), the outfits I bought at Macy's (white linen suit for me, Hawaiian shirt and khaki shorts for Armando), the game show on television when we picked up the package for Sonny Tzoc's brother (Wheel of Fortune), the birthday gift Armando's mother gave him when we stopped to see her in Reedley (canister of mace), the ethnicity of my parents' housekeeper in Newport Beach (African American), and the beat goes on.

So what's the rub, you ask. Why am I here? Please, no metaphysical questions.

The rub is not Armando's memory per se. Armando's memory per se is fine. He used to memorize pages and pages of notes before tests and even years later he could quote entire stanzas of *Paradise Lost* or whatever. I've fried way too many brain cells to dispute his recollection of particular events. If he said it happened, it happened. But something else may have happened too. Armando dwells on details and skimps on context, background, juicy gossip.

That's where I come in. I carry a laptop.

During college Armando wrote the worst poetry. He double majored in English and Spanish, and all that literature exercised a terrible influence. I hate his fat style, the way he lays extra phrases on every sentence, until they thicken and thicken, like this. I hate his pretentious epigraphs.

Don't get me wrong. It's not easy to tell the truth. I give Armando credit for trying. I just wish he'd majored in history or anthropology or political silence. I mean *science.* He could have provided more depth.

Which brings us back to *moi.* Armando asked me to critique his manuscript and fill in the gaps. Let's just say I feel compelled to oblige. In the case of this second chapter, there happen to be enough gaps that I'm simply replacing his version with my own.

So. Without further ado. Maestro, a little background music, please.

Once upon a time, when I first visited Guatemala, the death squads were planting corpses everywhere. I rented a Land Rover and headed for the boondocks, but no matter which highway I took, I'd hit a roadblock and a squad of gun-crazy soldier boys would turn me back. I lobbied all sorts of officials but couldn't get permission to visit most areas, much less do fieldwork. After three months, in desperation, I finally followed my father's advice and looked up one of his old cronies, a coffee baron named Hoover Schultz.

Background on background: Most of Guatemala's substantial German populace lost their property during World War II. The government just confiscated it. Only two families had enough clout to keep everything, and the Schultz clan was one of them. They owned a coffee plantation on the *boca costa* and a furniture factory in Antigua, and they held a major interest in one of the leading banks in the capital.

Hoover and my father had been fraternity brothers at Boston College in the 1940s and business associates in Guatemala in the 1950s. Hoover, for reasons of his own, idolized my father and couldn't do enough for me. He wangled me a distinguished-guest-of-the-republic card signed by the President and had me introduced to his coffee pickers, who became the subject of my dissertation.

Once I started my fieldwork, I avoided Hoover. The only times I saw him were after each coup—he'd give me a new card signed by the new President.

As for his lovely daughter, I met her once in passing—she mispronounced my name and dashed off to flute practice. The whole time I was in the field, I assumed she was a snob.

Afterwards, though, when I returned to Guatemala to fact-check my dissertation, one of my informants asked me to convince Hoover to permit an election among the coffee pickers. I didn't think Hoover would like the idea, but I dropped in on him anyway, and while I was waiting outside his study, Magdalena brought me a glass of iced tea with a sprig of fresh mint, and we talked. Later that day, when I picked up my mail at American Express and learned I'd been offered a teaching job, Magdalena was the person I wanted to celebrate with.

The point is that my father more or less brought us together. He made our match. I'd missed him when I'd called from Guatemala with the big news—he was out golfing, my mother had said. She herself had sounded oddly distracted. In shock, I assumed, at the whirlwinditude of the courtship.

Anyway, when Armando and I drove into Newport Beach, I

had visions of proud speeches, tearful hugs, and mended fences. Armando's version slights this context. So it's up to me to tell the sordid tale. Properly.

We arrived at my parents' house late Saturday afternoon. My mother kissed my cheek and criticized my beard. "A gentleman would shave that scratchy thing," she said, a hint of Southern lilt in her voice. My mother is tall and hyperthin, as precariously graceful as a flamingo. (Per Armando.) She was wearing a tennis skirt and a pale red sweater that matched her hair and her wine spritzer.

"There are no gentlemen in this family," I said. "Speaking of which—where's the old man?"

My brother was talking business on the phone. "I'll be through with this asshole in a minute," he said, ever the sentimentalist.

"Your father's had a little heart attack," my mother said. Then she immediately added, "*Relax*. He's been home from the hospital for a week now. He's practically his crabby old self."

I refused the drink she tried to serve me. "When I called from Guatemala, you said he was at the *golf course!*"

"I didn't want to spoil your good news." She beeped the sickroom on the intercom. "Why don't you go back and see him?"

"This is typical of my family," I said to Armando, who studiously scrutinized his wine spritzer.

"I can just hang out in the living room," he said.

"Not on your life," I said. "In for a nickel, in for a dime."

The sickroom smelled of rubbing alcohol, chrysanthemums, and Brylcream. My father was vigorously trying to turn off the TV with the control to the mechanical bed. He pressed every button at least twice. "I've got too damn many controls," he said, half laughing, half crying at his own frustration. The petite Korean nurse turned off the TV and readjusted the bed before discreetly leaving us alone.

"I'm really sorry about the heart attack," I said, taking my father's almost weightless hand.

"You think *you're* sorry?" He winked at Armando, who plastered a pleasant smile on his face and blended into the background. Armando should have been an anthropologist. He has a knack for noticing things without being noticed.

"How're you feeling?" I said. "You don't look so bad."

"Please—put it nicer," my father said. "Check out my new Italian bathrobe. Spiffy, huh?"

"What's the word from the doctors? Are you well enough to travel?"

"Travel?" my father said. He stroked my fingers. "You mean the wedding deal? I guess your mother hasn't clued you in yet."

I pulled back my hand.

"It wasn't my decision," my father said. "You know how your mother loathes the Latin countries. Hell, she won't go anywhere there's not a tennis tournament or a sexy guru."

I swayed over to the ficus in the corner. "They skipped my graduations and crap when I was a kid," I explained to Armando. "But my wedding. Correction: my wedding *deal.* I presumed they might care to see that."

"Maybe I can take a little sting out of the wound," my father said. "That envelope on the dresser is for you."

I picked up the ficus by the upper branches and slammed it against the wall. The terra cotta pot smashed into pieces.

Armando shuddered, but my father didn't even blink. "Chill out," he said. "Your mother's planning a big shindig for after the honeymoon. She's reserved the Kamehameha Room at the club."

"I may be busy then. I'm moving to Connecticut, it so happens. I have a *new job* to get ready for, a *book* to revise."

My father groped around the bedside table, knocked off a box of Kleenex and a *Fortune* magazine, then latched onto a bottle of pills, which he labored urgently to uncap, at last shaking a tiny tablet onto his tongue and washing it down with hasty gulps of water.

If he meant to remind me of the nearness of death and of his meager defenses against it, he succeeded. I rushed over and dabbed his forehead with a cool washcloth.

"Would you do something for me?" he asked.

"Of course," I said, although now that the crisis had passed, I felt a little leery.

"Would you give me some of that Jap massage?"

I couldn't help grinning. "The word is *shiatsu.*"

He took off his robe and his silk pajama top. I climbed on the bed and straddled him. "Be gentle," he said. He groaned with pleasure as I pressed my thumbs into his back. Armando sipped his spritzer.

"You could at least feel guilty about disappointing me," I said, applying and releasing pressure.

"Shut up and rub," my father said, but he said it almost sweetly.

"I figured you'd be jazzed," I said. "Here I am marrying the daughter of your great Guatemalan *amigo.* You practically fixed us up."

His back tensed. "How come your hands are so smart and your brain's so dumb?"

"Didn't you beg me to cultivate Hoover? Didn't you brag about his clout?"

"Maybe that was a mistake," he said.

"I thought Hoover was your main man."

"I love Hoover like a brother, but you don't choose your brothers."

I eased off his back. "You mean you don't like him? You don't approve?"

My father rolled over and sat up. He puffed out his flabby pink chest as if there were medals pinned on it. "You know I'm not a snob," he said. "Hoover's a fine gentleman and a very valuable friend, but he can be a little bumpkinish at times, a little overzealous. He'll do so much for you, you feel like you owe him, and he's not a person you want to owe. If I was the kind of father who gave advice—"

"Hah!" I said.

"I'd advise you to steer as clear of Hoover as possible. Don't let him do you any favors. If you need something, I'm your man."

I climbed off the bed. "All I want from Hoover is his daughter. Wait. I did ask him one favor, an election for his coffee pickers, but he nixed that."

"Then you're lucky. Every favor is a debt as far as Hoover is concerned. My father-in-law was exactly the same. *Listen to me. Are you too damn stupid to listen?*" My father blinked back tears, as if a lifetime's worth of anguish suddenly threatened to overwhelm him.

I had turned my attention to the fig tree again, plucking its leaves and dropping them. "I'm listening," I said. "I just don't like what I hear. This marriage was supposed to please you, but all you've done is bitch."

"I have not yet begun to bitch," my father said. "The doctors hanker after my gonads. My smart-ass son has his head in the clouds and his feet in a pile of crap. Put that in your pipe and smoke it." My father reached down to the foot of the bed for his eagle-headed cane and pointed it at me. "Question. Are you sure you want to marry this girl?"

I froze in mid-pluck.

"I've spent a lot of time in other countries," my father said. "It's easy to get swept off your feet. It's like a fairy tale. And you're the handsome prince. You meet a sexy maiden, and naturally you want to do the right thing. Live happily ever after. Only sometimes, after the mystique wears off, it ain't that happy. You're stuck with different languages, different customs, different families."

I gawked at my father, just plain gawked.

"I'll only ask you once," he went on. "I won't bring this up again. But how well do you really know her? How much do you have in common? Remember, a marriage is not a romantic proposition. Hot in the pants means diddly-squat in the long run."

"Thanks for your concern," I said. "Your wisdom falls like rain upon a parched land."

"If I've hurt your feelings, I'm sorry. All I'm trying to get across is that it's okay to change your mind. Your mother and I will support you either way. Understand? We only want what's best for you. If you're happy, we're happy."

"I'm happy," I said. I pressed the flat of my hand against my forehead.

"Good." He pointed at the envelope on the dresser. "There should be enough to finance quite a honeymoon—or whatever else your heart desires."

"My heart desires *you*. At my wedding. With a flower in your lapel. Looking proud. But forget it. I didn't realize your health was failing."

"My health is fine. I still sign the checks around here. I still pay the bills. Your mother vetoed this one. Work on *her*."

"No, your condition matters a lot more than my wedding. Death is scary. Admit it."

"My heart muscle is in great shape. It's just the arteries are clogged. Too much good living. Now grab that cash and blow."

"No thanks."

"Why the hell not?"

"I don't like the strings attached."

"Ten thousand smackers cut a lot of string."

"I'm touched beyond words. Sincerely. But I must decline."

"Armando, would you hang on to that envelope until Patrick wises up?"

Armando's glass was empty, he discovered when he tried to drink. He poured himself some water and slowly sipped.

"Armando would rather stay out of this," I said.

"Who wouldn't?" my father said. He pointed first at Armando, then at the envelope.

"Maybe what's important is that you love each other," Armando said. "That's why you care about each other's opinion so much." He paused as if he intended to say more, but I put my finger down my throat and my father played an invisible violin.

"Who's this pal of yours? Pollyanna? He's a riot."

"A veritable sage," I said. My father and I grinned at each other so hard my mouth hurt. "Look, I'll accept your money, but not as a gift. That was a ten thousand dollar massage."

At dinner my brother talked powerboats with Armando while I confronted my mother.

"It's not me," she said. "It's your father."

"He claims different."

"Of course. He's in a stage of denial."

"I thought you said he was his crabby old self."

"That's how he wants us to treat him, Patrick."

"If he agreed to go—"

"He's in no condition. My friend Fiona brought him flowers yesterday, and she told me his aura's the worst she's ever seen."

"A trip might do him good," I said.

"He just had his fourth coronary. He's been diagnosed with prostate cancer. The doctors recommend surgery as soon as he regains enough strength."

"He was fine at Christmas."

"Sometimes it strikes all at once," my mother said. "Especially a man like your father. He's ignored his body for years, ignored the signs of weakness. Fiona says you create what you fear the most, and he fears losing power, losing control—"

"Losing hair," my brother interrupted dismissively. "He's a pip. He'll outlive all of us."

"You're denying, just like he is," my mother said.

"Mark my words," my brother said. "Rumors of the old spook's demise are greatly exaggerated."

"Speaking of my wedding," I said with a theatrical cough.

"What's the big deal?" my brother said. "We'll party right here in a couple weeks."

"If you'll excuse me," my mother said, rising quickly. "I need to check on our patient."

Armando, my brother, and I adjourned to the hot tub after dinner. We sipped cognac from enormous snifters. A three-quarter moon lit the stretch of beach between the patio and the Pacific. My brother snorted cocaine and knocked academia, which he called *school.*

"School is fine. In its place. Like the army. Or religion. But you don't join the priesthood. What's your specialty? Toe jam of the Third World?"

I waved away the coke spoon. "You have no idea what it's like down there. People dig the earth with sticks and plant beans by hand while you indulge every orifice of your body."

"Luck of the draw," my brother said.

"It's not luck," I said.

"You mean it's my fault I was born here?"

"I mean that your wealth and their poverty are two sides of the same coin. This hot tub and this cognac depend on their illiteracy and malnutrition."

My brother has a way of listening that must serve him well in the courtrooms of Orange County. His eyes aimed upward, his jaw went slack, his lips drooped in utter boredom. But he paid attention.

"That's a mighty big generalization," he said. "How about some facts?"

"It's not an easy connection to explain," I said.

"I bet," he said.

I sat up on the ledge that rimmed half the hot tub. "My *campesinos* pick coffee beans for three bucks a day. If they were paid even a fourth of our minimum wage, imagine what a cup of coffee would cost. Coffee, cotton, cocaine—it all depends on peasants virtually starving on beans and tortillas. That's exploitation, as far as I'm concerned."

"Listen, Leon Trotsky, call it what you will, but good businessmen take advantage of every opportunity. That's what being on top means. You want some Red Chinese soaking his butt here beside the ocean? You want some Arab sheik? Because there's always going to be somebody delecting the grape at the expense of somebody else bent over in the fields."

"You really see the connection? Most Americans don't realize—"

"Everyone knows the dirty work gets done. Hell, it sent *us* to the finest universities. Where do you think your trust fund comes from?"

"Another family mystery I'd like to get to the bottom of."

"Ignorance is bliss, baby brother." He ran his hand through his thinning hair.

"Suppose the President showed up right now," I said. "Suppose he brought a Guatemalan peasant with him. Blindfolded. With his hands tied behind his back. And the President said, 'If you want to keep this redwood hot tub and this vintage cognac, you have to put a bullet right between this peasant's eyes. Just aim right here. Go ahead. Shoot.' Could you do it? Could you kill him just to keep your fine things? Because I doubt if I could."

My brother boosted himself onto the ledge beside me. "Don't be too sure," he said. I searched his eyes for a glimmer of humor. "Don't be too sure."

Wisps of steam curled into the darkness. My brother opened his mouth without speaking and I actually thought he might dredge up a word of congratulations. No chance, of course. It's funny—only your family can fool you just by doing what they always do.

The moon neared the top of its arc, the ocean broke into silvery whitecaps, and along the moonlit beach came jogging three teenage girls in skimpy shorts and halter tops. Giggling, giddy Newport Beach Lolitas, with tender, mouth-watering thighs. The surf lapped at their feet. Not a bad moment to share with your brother and your best friend.

"I'm in love," my brother said.

"No, you're in lust," I said.

"I'm serious," my brother said. "I'm in love with my secretary."

"Which one is *she*?" I said. I was still watching the girls.

"Forget that jailbait," my brother said. He chopped the water with his forearm. Armando looked anywhere but at us.

"What about your wife?" I said.

"My secretary saved my life," my brother said.

"Has she asked you to get a divorce?"

"No. She's asked me to leave her alone. She says it's wrong."

"Wrong." The word surprised me. I had a low opinion of my brother's moral development, and yet, man that I am, I automatically assumed the worst about his secretary, scheming to sink her hooks into his money. Knee-jerk sexism? *Nolo contendere.* "Who came on to who?" I said.

"She would never come on. I practically attacked her one night we worked late together. She shut me down cold. She told me what a decent man I was, how I wouldn't want to take advantage of her. I figured she was playing hard to get, but she wasn't playing. After a couple months went by, she gave notice.

I *demanded* she stay, but she just laughed, not mean—more a life-sure-is-crazy kind of thing. I kissed her. I wanted to fuck her right there on my desk, but she wouldn't let me. We flew to Phoenix and stayed at the Hilton just for the afternoon. That's how discreet she is. She's got a kid. Same age as mine."

"How old is this woman?"

"Her name is Angelica Flores. Angel flowers. Isn't that beautiful?"

"Yeah, beautiful. So what year was she born?"

"I suppose she's twenty-five. Twenty-four, maybe. Twenty-three and a half. She's not Mex. She's Argentine. No offense, Armando."

"None taken," Armando said.

"How long have you been seeing her?" I said.

"I've been seeing her for months, but the Phoenix deal was the only sex. Sometimes I'm afraid it was a dream. I asked her last week, 'Did it really happen?' and she took my hand and kissed it, and that kept me *sane*. I've begged her to let me set her up in a nice apartment, but she says I have a wife and a kid already, and she has a kid too, and it wouldn't be right."

"It wouldn't be right," I repeated, as if my brother had used an obscure foreign phrase. "So what are you going to do?"

"I need advice," my brother said. "I've never been this desperate."

"How's your marriage going?" I said.

"We get along," my brother said, "but she's no Angelica."

"Aren't we talking marriage?" I said. "The sacred institution? If we were talking cars, I could understand. Everyone wants a new car."

"I want *her*," my brother said.

"You want this year's model of *her*. Our Lady of Perpetual Youth."

My brother hauled himself out of the hot tub. He poked Armando in the shoulder with his toe. "This is the peckerwood who once planted a microphone in our parents' bedroom because he wanted to find out what they did in there. He was sure they never did it. Is he this righteous with you?"

Armando clasped his hands behind his head. "Well, when I

told him a woman at work kind of liked me, he said, 'Follow her into the bathroom and shove your tongue down her throat.'"

"That's because *you* have moral sense," I said. "*He* has the moral sense of a lawyer, for God's sake."

"So what do you think I should do, Armando?" my brother said.

"I'm not the one to ask," Armando said.

"None of this humbler-than-thou routine. Help me."

Armando slapped a handful of water against the back of his neck. "Sometimes what you do every day can seem like a trap—"

"Exactly!" my brother said. He didn't wait for Armando to finish his thought. "I'm breaking out of a trap. One thing has me worried, though. What if she loses interest? Her husband's dead, but if she took up with another man, I swear I'd kill him."

"It seems a bit premature to plot the murder of your hypothetical mistress's hypothetical lover," I said. "You'll ruin your crime-of-passion defense."

"She's not a hypothetical mistress. She's a hypothetical wife."

"You're married, for Christ's sake."

"A wise fox never leaves his hole until he's found another," my brother said.

"No. No," I said. "That's too crude even for you."

"Are you kidding?" my brother said. "The old man imparted those words of wisdom to me when I divorced Jeannette eight years ago."

"You lie," I said.

"I don't lie," my brother said. He'd been sitting on the ledge of the hot tub and now he stood up, steaming. "You're just afraid of what's inside you. The crude McGuffin blood. Wait till your metabolism changes. Wait till your cheeks puff out and your nose turns red and your belly sags over your belt. Wait till your breath stinks in the morning. And then when some sweet sophomore stays after class and begs for extra credit, don't get crude. Blood rules, bro'. Your righteous days are almost through."

Armando and I sat so still in the hot tub that the water stopped moving. The surface became a mirror of murky shapes. I don't know what I saw there, but I had one of those rare generous impulses, especially rare in my family. "Why don't you come to Guatemala with us?" I said to my brother. "We'll ride the bus to Lake Atitlán. Mix with the multitudes. See the shrunken old women and the crippled beggars and the dark schoolgirls in blue skirts and white socks."

"If I had the time . . ." my brother said, and then he grinned. "If I had the time, I still wouldn't ride a fucking bus."

Armando's version omits the part of the conversation that had to do with sex, maybe because he was afraid it might offend his mother. I love Armando's mother, but you can't be totally honest with your mother reading over your shoulder all the time.

Let's face it. Armando is a prude. He bowdlerized his memories before he wrote them down.

A memory, no matter how accurate, is not like a photograph or a tape recording. There are no untouched proofs. The original perception is already distorted by attitude. Your frame of mind defines the boundaries of your vision from the get-go. Armando's recollections are colored by his prudity—mine, by my crudity.

No, it's more than that. It's the whole system of values. Armando assumes the best about everyone, even my family. He probably tuned out my conversation with my brother because it seemed too unflattering to be true.

But I couldn't tune it out. I felt cursed. I feel cursed now.

One last thing in contradiction of Armando. Ice may turn to water, and water to steam, but it's still H_2O. Which means that if you've got the crude McGuffin blood in your veins, you're doomed to be a crude McGuffin for life.

III

PERSPECTIVE

But in order to go on, it is necessary to go back.

LAWRENCE DURRELL

My wife, Betsy, had the ability not to think, and I envied that. I remember when she was working in Hartman's Bookstore six days a week to help put me through law school, how sometimes at night she'd ask me to come sit with her and I'd resent the intrusion. Reluctantly, I'd join her on the couch, she'd drop her magazine, and I'd want to pick it up and read it, as if I couldn't afford to stop processing information even for a second. What a sacrifice I believed I was making, allowing my wife to snuggle her shoulder under my arm, where it fit perfectly, and letting time go by. I'd fret about my class work, which assignment to do next, but Betsy, for those long minutes, wouldn't think about anything. She swore her mind went blank when she relaxed: it was like turning off a radio or tuning it where there was no station. What about the static, I asked. She told me I had to learn not to think all the time, but I didn't know how not to think, and I couldn't figure it out—until Spoon and I got stuck in Mexico City.

It was supposed to be a thirty-minute layover, but the pressure lock lost its pressure, and so the plane, with all passengers aboard, held itself hostage next to the terminal for three and a half hours.

At first I was aggravated. Spoon was busy proofreading his dissertation. I read my Rilke book and then just stared out the window. It was raining. The sky was gray, the runway was gray, the planes taking off and landing were gray. I checked my watch twice before I realized that I was in no hurry. I'd already caught the plane I needed to catch. A man in a yellow raincoat and yellow rainboots splashed across a wide puddle. I heard the steady spatter of rain above me, and for a moment I lost all awareness. For a moment my failure of a marriage, my unfulfilling job, my heavy body, even the complicated traumas of my family didn't exist or didn't matter. There was no static. Thought simply stopped.

If perspective is a distance that reveals the true relationship of things, then the distance Spoon and I had traveled these past two days provided the perspective I needed. Stranded on this wet tarmac halfway between San Francisco and Guatemala City, I saw the constraints of my old life and I felt free of them. I had come here by choice; I could leave and go wherever I wanted. Certain restrictions applied, of course. It said so on my ticket. After my blissful instant of not thinking, I acknowledged the restrictions. I acknowledged Reedley.

It used to be so easy going home. When my father was alive and I was in college, there were problems, sure, but they weren't my problems. I saw my parents' unfortunate marriage, but I didn't see how hard it was to live with the same person year after year. I saw my grandparents getting older, but I didn't see the gathering momentum of decrepitude and death. I suppose I wore the blinders of youth.

Spoon and I had spent only an hour in Reedley on our way to Newport Beach, but even a single minute would have evoked the entire haunted history of my family. Every word, every gesture mangled my heart. My mother had waited on us at Bodine's Coffee Shop. She'd tried to trade shifts, but Donna Rae, the other waitress, was out with hay fever.

"At least you'll get wonderful service," my mother had said, smiling. She has a great smile, part shy and girlish, part motherly wise.

My mother is a woman who lives from crisis to crisis. When she doesn't have one of her own, she borrows. "You absolutely cannot go!" she insisted as soon as she filled our water glasses.

"Please don't start," I said.

"It's dangerous," she said. "Mary Pritchard's sister spent two weeks in El Salvador with the Methodist Church. Nuns have been shot, according to her."

"We'll be extremely careful, Mrs. Santiesteban," Spoon said. He scooted over to let my mother slide in next to him. She wore a green name tag that said "Izzy," even though her name is Isabel, a beautiful name, in my opinion.

She took my hand and looked me in the eyes. She believes in

looking people in the eyes. "I can't make this decision for you," she said.

"Thank heaven for small favors," I said.

She hauled herself to her feet. "The one ray of sunshine is, the Rotary Club wants to hear all about it."

"Are you serious?"

"Luncheon meeting. Three Wednesdays from next week. I've already arranged everything with Mr. Berryman." She fiddled with my collar. "Who irons your shirts?" she said.

We ate patty melts and fries. My mother took orders, poured coffee, carried dishes to and from the service ledge. Her walk had changed since my last visit, become slower and stiffer. She still held her back straight and her chin level, but she put her weight down more deliberately, as if each step hurt. She'd gained five pounds a year since my father died, she smoked half a pack a day, and recently she'd developed shinsplints to go with her high blood pressure. Nevertheless, when she sank into our booth again, she lit a Kool and told us that she was the happiest woman in the world.

"I wish I had your strength," Spoon said.

"I wish I had your car," she said, and we laughed. Spoon's vintage Mustang was parked outside our window next to my mother's crunched Maverick. "I don't know *what* I'm going to do! It's *absolutely* beyond repair!" She threw her head back and blew an anguished cloud of smoke.

"What about Donna Rae's Toyota?" I said.

"It's a stick," she said. "I don't even like the way that sounds."

"You can learn to drive a stick," I said.

"I'm not mechanical enough. And I'd be a sitting duck in that little thing."

"You want a tank?" I said.

"Your sister, if she ever gets here, is taking me car shopping in Fresno this afternoon."

"Dolores doesn't know cars."

"I need to see my grandson. I never see my grandson."

While we waited for Dolores, my mother brought us two huge pieces of hot rhubarb pie smothered with vanilla ice cream — unordered, of course. How could I tell her I was trying to cut down?

"We'll run you over to Fresno," Spoon said after swallowing his last bite.

"Oh, no, dear. That's very kind, but your parents are expecting you."

My mother cleared our plates. Spoon put a twenty under the salt shaker, but I pushed it back at him.

"Let her treat," I said.

"We can't stiff your mother," he said.

We played tug-of-war in reverse with our fingers on the twenty, and my mother caught us. It was nearly two o'clock. The lunch rush was over. She set down her bulky macramé handbag, took off her name tag, and unpinned her long, silver-black hair. "Is that a donation to the church bazaar?" she finally said. Dear Abby herself couldn't have solved the problem better.

Outside, by Spoon's Mustang, my mother worked the conversation around to the Rotary Club again.

"You're such a good son," she said. "And you do so much for me. It would make me very proud if you talked to them. Some of the boys you went to high school with are in Rotary now. And they serve a wonderful lunch."

"I won't have time," I said. "Besides, I don't eat chicken-fried steak." I retied my shoes on the bumper of the Mustang. The seams of my mother's stockings, I noticed, lined up perfectly. Her cheap white skirt and blouse shimmered with a hint of rainbow colors in the sunlight.

Luckily, my sister Dolores zipped into the parking lot in her Mazda RX7; unluckily, she failed to bring her son, Jason.

"Where's my pride and joy?" my mother said.

"Jason has his piano lesson today," Dolores said. "You know that."

My mother wiped her eyes with one of my father's red bandannas. Spoon began to tell her about his fiancée.

Meanwhile, Dolores kissed me on each cheek — not a family custom — and held me at arm's length. There was something different about her too, something not quite right about her face.

Her nose had been reshaped. I fumbled for the appropriate response to my sister's plastic surgery: a compliment? discreet silence? indiscreet silence? Dolores has been beautiful since birth. She has my mother's thick black hair and luminous brown eyes. It would be foolish of me to praise my father's nose, but changing it had not increased Dolores's beauty, not to my mind at least.

"I love you, little sister," I said in Spanish, but she took the use of Spanish as a rebuke. I hadn't meant it that way—or maybe I had. She'd never learned much Spanish. She stayed out of the sun as much as possible and wore makeup to lighten her skin. In fact, until she became Dolores Alexander, she'd worked as a makeup artist at Merle Norman in Fresno and lightened the skin of other Latinas.

When she dropped my hands, I had to wonder if the touch of my sweaty palms offended her.

"You love me, but you disapprove," she said. "I hate the way you judge me from a distance, Armando. I do all I can for Izzy, but she's turned into a leech. You don't have to deal with it up in San Francisco, but she's helpless *on purpose.* 'I need you, dear.' That's what she always says to me. She wants Jason to be *her son,* and I can't stand it anymore. If Bart gets this transfer to South Carolina, we're moving for sure."

My sister's eyes blazed, but her outburst reminded me of our most joyous squabbles. I smiled until she gave in to my unexpected surge of good humor.

"Isn't Armando looking fantastic?" she said for my mother's benefit. "A few more pounds and he'll be a certified hunk again. You should find out his diet secrets, Mom."

"I'll never lose this weight," my mother said. "What should I tell Mr. Berryman?" she asked me.

"Tell him I'll consider his invitation as soon as my mother learns how to drive a standard."

"Listen to your smart son," Dolores said. "Donna Rae's car would solve all your problems."

"I want a Granada," my mother said. "I deserve a Granada."

"That's salesman talk," Dolores said. "You can't afford a Granada."

"With the insurance on the Maverick plus my retirement fund—"

"Forget insurance."

"But it wasn't my fault."

"It was nobody's fault, but this family has no luck with insurance," Dolores said.

My father's insurance company had contested the nature of his death as accidental. My mother had settled out of court for less than the value of the policy.

"Am I naive?" my mother said. She ran my father's bandanna across her forehead and around her neck, which drew my attention to the age lines there. I realized how tired she must feel, how tired of being Izzy.

I lightly kissed the dimple on her cheek and she rested her head against my chest for a second.

"Stay out of harm's way," she said.

"He'll be safer in Guatemala than he would be in a car with you," Dolores said.

It was only a joke, but my mother took it wrong.

"Yes," she said. "No one in our family should drive."

And just like that the death of my father surrounded us.

My mother unearthed a gift-wrapped package from the rubble of her handbag. "Don't open it now. You'll complain, and I don't need complaints."

I shook the box. I held it to my forehead like a psychic. "It's perfect," I said. "I wanted a snakebite kit. Or is it one of those money belts you wear under your shirt?"

My mother knew I was clowning for her sake, but she refused to play along. I touched the spot between her ribs that always made her laugh, and she started crying.

"Promise me you'll keep it with you at all times," she said.

Behind her, my sister arched her dark eyebrows. See how she's manipulating you, the look said.

"I promise," I said.

"I'm so lucky to have such a wonderful son," my mother said. "Your wonderful brother wished he could be here, but the honor society picnic is this afternoon. The teachers say he's a shoo-in for Stanford."

"Tell him to enjoy himself," I said.

"Tell him to do anything Armando wouldn't do," Spoon said.

As he eased the Mustang out of Bodine's parking lot, my mother put her arm around my sister and they waved good-bye. My sister's gold bracelets broke the light into dazzling rays. The red bandanna in my mother's hand flapped briefly and then hung straight.

In Mexico City, watching plane after cumbersome plane lift itself into the sky, I saw the possibility of change. For years I had believed that I deserved to suffer. A lapse of discipline had ruined my life and the best I could do was resign myself to it. There was no other choice. But this gray interregnum gave me a new perspective. I realized how utterly I'd wallowed in my problems. They weren't the result of a past mistake—I created them fresh every day and willfully avoided the most obvious solutions. My mother wouldn't learn how to drive a stick, and I wouldn't shift gears either. Looking at the world through a rain-spattered window, I decided that it might be possible to change myself a little, to become, if not carefree, at least somewhat less careful.

On our flight to Guatemala City, I fell into a deep, dream-laden sleep that lasted until Spoon shifted my seat back into the upright position. "The butterfly emerges from its cocoon," he said as I blinked my eyes unstuck. My wave of gusto had passed. Spoon, though, more than compensated for my lack. As soon as the wheels bumped against the runway, he snatched his suit from the overhead compartment and dashed for the door. He was the first passenger off the plane.

I trudged after him in a zombie-like trance. I wasn't ready to be anywhere yet. I couldn't analyze my impressions; I could only register the threadbare brown carpet, the antiseptic cherry smell, the ghostly whir of empty conveyor belts. Spoon saved a place for me at the front of the customs line. I don't know if he relied on bribery or charm, but we got our passports stamped and our bags waved through ahead of everyone else.

I followed him past the obvious exit and down a short corridor. He vaulted over a turnstile and I climbed over. Nothing seemed quite in focus until he dug an elbow into my shoulder and pointed toward the far end of the terminal where a young woman was sitting absolutely still, absolutely tranquil, as if she possessed the wisdom of infinite patience. Even in my stupefaction I recognized her ability not to think.

"Behold," Spoon said with proprietary zeal.

She had black hair cut short in a boyish mop-top that tricked me into seeing her as cute instead of beautiful. She wore a white sleeveless blouse, new blue jeans, and purple sneakers. On the chair next to her lay a paperback, a *Bride* magazine, and a crossword puzzle, distractions she'd evidently discarded in favor of not thinking. Spoon and I admired at closer and closer range her serious eyebrows, her strong cheekbones, her slender but muscular arms. We were almost ready to bow at her feet when the low growl of a dog froze both of us.

Magdalena blinked herself into the present moment and, with breathtaking grace, slowly rose. Her expression had a certain sleepy quality that stopped my heart. She spoke in Spanish to her German shepherd. "Calm down, *Tía Marta.*" Then, in English, she said to me: "My constant chaperon, Aunt Martha. She's much better company than the average bodyguard."

With no enthusiasm whatsoever I held out my hand for Aunt Martha to sniff while Spoon bent low to receive Magdalena's brief kiss on the cheek.

"I'm so glad to see you," he said.

Their restraint surprised me. Spoon's last girlfriend used to jump into his arms and wrap her legs around his waist just to say hi.

"I'm afraid we should hurry," Magdalena said as she stowed her things in her purse.

"Hurry?" Spoon said. "We just got here."

"There's a reception in our honor," Magdalena said. "We're already late."

"Do you want to go to a reception?" Spoon asked me. "Do you?" he asked Magdalena.

She shrugged as if what she wanted was of no concern.

"A flight delayed three hours can be delayed four," Spoon said. "We can go drink beer at Albóndigas."

"My father would know," Magdalena said. "The Omniscient One knows all." She surveyed the whole terminal, as if even the man selling chiclets might be her father's spy.

"I don't mind going to a reception in our honor," Spoon said. "But the point is we have a choice."

"Ah," Magdalena said, with a teasing smile. "We are being theoretic."

"Theoretic. Yes," Spoon said. He excused himself and took his duffel with him.

Magdalena scratched Aunt Martha behind the ears. I can't explain why, but I sensed that she was hiding disappointment.

"Aunt Martha likes to be petted on the rump," she said. "Is that the right word, *petted?*"

"I think so. It sounds funny, doesn't it?"

We both petted Aunt Martha for a while. Magdalena asked about our flight. I complimented her dangly earrings. We made polite conversation until Spoon sauntered back, completely transformed. He'd washed his face, combed his hair, and changed into his new white suit.

I gestured at what I was wearing, the garish outfit he'd foisted on me at Macy's, flip-flops, khaki shorts, Hawaiian shirt emblazoned with dolphins.

"Understated elegance," Spoon said. "The ultimate fashion statement."

He put his arm around Magdalena. Aunt Martha and I brought up the rear. The combination of Spoon at six-six and Magdalena at just over five feet struck me as more than averagely awkward. I thought to myself how, when two people first walk with their arms around each other, their bodies don't necessarily fit. They learn, gradually, where to support and where to give. Spoon and Magdalena hadn't learned to fit together yet. I have to admit I envied them the learning.

And then the chaos began, the outstretched hands of anguished beggars, grim young soldiers brandishing m-14s, authentic Mayan artifacts for sale cheap, jackhammers, sirens, the smell of car exhaust and fry bread and unwashed human bodies. All of a sudden I felt the trip taking *me*, the way a river might take a rudderless raft.

Perched on the backseat of Magdalena's battleship of a Buick, I didn't just look—I tried to memorize the endless sprawl of Guatemala City, the sheet-metal shacks and swank department stores, tree-lined plazas and monumental statues. I had to force myself not to stare at the Indians, the dark, distant, petroglyphic Indians, their faces so devoid of light, their clothes so resplendent, especially the women's magnificent blouses bursting with geometric flecks of color as vivid as any masterpiece by Gauguin or van Gogh.

Spoon provided a running commentary. "See that crack? That's the 1976 earthquake."

Magdalena kept her eyes on the road while Spoon pointed out buzzards and black marketeers and cardboard lean-tos braced against the high whitewashed walls surrounding the grandest mansions on Avenida Goya. Most of the walls were topped with barbed wire. The barbed wire on one wall was laced with red and green Christmas lights glowing faintly in the late afternoon sunshine.

"My favorite landmark," Spoon said.

An armed guard waved us through the wrought-iron gates of Casa Schultz. We weaved among the polished limousines and dented clunkers parked pell-mell in the circular driveway. Several chauffeurs, some barefoot, kicked around an empty can.

I was a little overwhelmed by the opulence and the proximity of its opposite extreme. Lagging behind Spoon and Magdalena, I shifted my heavy Samsonite from hand to hand. I could have dragged it by the strap, but I didn't want to embarrass Spoon. My duty was to be a good best man.

IV

THE GUITAR IS MISSING

Your true enemy resides in your very own house.
GUATEMALAN PROVERB

Permit me a generalization. Mexican men don't wear shorts. Women and children and worthless idlers might indulge in such foolishness, but not true Mexican men. My father, for instance, on the occasions my family vacationed at Pismo Beach or Lake Nacimiento, wore his usual green overalls and hard-soled black shoes. It's almost perverse that of all the things I could have learned from my father—skepticism, silence, strength of will—I picked up the habit of not wearing shorts. I mention this because Spoon, long-legged Spoon, loved shorts. On our whirlwind shopping spree at Macy's, he'd pushed hard for pink polka dots, but I'd drawn the line at khaki.

I might as well have been wearing polka dots, though, for all the mortification I felt standing in the immense doorway of Casa Schultz. It was as bad as my law school nightmares of rushing into class naked.

Magdalena's father, Hoover Schultz, a short wide bull of a man, pumped my hand and slapped my back. I probably should have thanked him for sporting an outfit louder than mine. His plaid sports coat barely contained his massive gut and meaty shoulders. His red pants would have drawn raves at the Reedley Municipal Golf Course. He directed the doorman to take our bags and herded Spoon and me over to the nearest group of guests.

"This is my distinguished future son-in-law, Dr. Patricio McGuffin, and his lifelong friend—" Hoover ransacked his memory at ruthless speed. "Armando Santiesteban. *Armando es un* Harvard Man."

I started to correct the misimpression, but Spoon interrupted. "Armando works for one of the most esteemed law firms in San Francisco," he said, grinning at me as if this were our little joke. I opened my mouth to protest but no words came out.

I met a wheelchair-bound colonel and his glamorous young wife, a cross-eyed judge, and a serene monsignor who said that Spoon and I reminded him of Don Quixote and Sancho Panza. When Hoover and Spoon moved on to the next group, I lingered.

"*Don Quixote* is my favorite novel in all literature," I said.

"I must read it someday," the monsignor said with dreamy good cheer. "I collect Quixotes. Paintings, carvings, etchings. Are you a man of art?"

Magdalena was kind enough to supply my answer. She'd parked Aunt Martha somewhere and changed into a simple white sundress that complimented her honey-colored skin. "I'm afraid Armando is a man of hunger at the moment."

"Then by all means, feed him," the monsignor said. His hands fluttered like birds caught in the sleeves of his cassock.

Magdalena led me to a long table covered with trays of stuffed mushrooms, goat cheese, and chicken wings. She served me a plate and found us an inconspicuous portion of wall to lean against. I'd been inside some impressive Boston houses, but Casa Schultz surpassed all of them in terms of sheer spectacle. Arched beams of burgundy wood formed a monumental dome over the center of the room. Hundreds of exquisite hand-painted tiles composed the floor. Unfortunately, the grand effect was undermined by seven larger-than-life religious portraits in which everything was overdone, the fleshiness of the flesh tones, the lollipop red blood, the sickly saintliness of the expressions, even the thickness of the gilt frames. And the maids wore tacky pink aprons and caps, the servant pouring the champagne held his pants up with a rope, and the old-fashioned hi-fi played the tinniest version of "Sentimental Journey" I'd ever heard.

"Patrick told me that you prefer to stand back," Magdalena said. "He does a rather amusing imitation of you." She stood at attention against the wall and clasped her hands on top of her head; it was funnier than I can describe to see this petite woman assume my air of stolid concentration.

"I guess I feel less likely to make a fool of myself," I said. I put my chewed chicken wing down on my plate, where it looked out of place, vulgar. Shreds of meat clung to the bone. I covered it with my napkin. "I'm not as brave as Patrick."

We looked across the room at Spoon in his Lord Jim suit enthusiastically demonstrating the fireside soft shoe he'd performed in the vacant lot in the Mission.

"I'm not that brave, either," Magdalena said.

And then someone let loose a high, trilling, mariachi yelp. A mature woman in a low-cut black dress sashayed around the champagne table and snatched a long-stemmed rose from a pewter vase. When Spoon started toward her, she clenched the rose between her teeth. They met each other halfway, under the apex of the dome. She gave him an exuberant tiptoe hug and he swung her into a fox-trot to the scratchy strains of "In the Mood."

"My mother acts much younger than her age," Magdalena said, turning her back on the display.

The woman in black didn't dance like a mother, not like my mother at least. No doubt she had once been as delicately slender as Magdalena, but over the years the curve of her hips and the swell of her thighs had become voluptuous. She coordinated her movements to Spoon's with a sexual ardor that revealed, in contrast, her daughter's reserve.

"Ever been to California?" I asked Magdalena, in an effort to provide a distraction.

Her smile wavered. "Once," she said.

"Did you get anywhere near Reedley? Fresno? The Central Valley?"

"A bit near, I think. My friend and I drove a van up the Highway 1."

There was something about the way she said *my friend,* a perceptible tenderness, a tremulous intake of breath. I felt jealous on Spoon's behalf, if that's possible.

"We saw redwoods and Mount Shasta and Hearst Castle and the Big Sur."

Beyond Magdalena, Spoon danced on with casual assurance. He let Magdalena's mother do most of the work, guiding her with gentle pressure to the lower back, a slight shift of the wrist. Beyond the two of them, Hoover drew his index finger across his throat. The servant stationed behind the champagne table moved to the hi-fi and waited for the song to end. Hoover made a more aggressive gesture: he jerked his whole arm across his throat. The servant immediately pulled the plug at the wall, so that the music wound down before it stopped.

Spoon and Magdalena's mother kept dancing. He played her out the length of his arm, she spun, he reeled her back to him and dipped her to the floor. They held that pose until people began to clap.

Hoover clapped only once. "Let's have some *real* music," he said. "Beto, bring Magdalena's flute."

Beto, the servant with the rope belt, didn't salute or click his heels, but he did turn at an abrupt right angle and march down the hall.

"Thank you for asking, Father," Magdalena said, even though he hadn't asked, "but I'm hopelessly unprepared."

"Nonsense," Hoover said. "Is there a single cretin here who would *not* be pleased to hear a selection from my loyal daughter?"

It's important to understand that Hoover had a sense of humor. He exaggerated his faults on purpose, as if to make them endearing. There's a phrase in Spanish, *cabeza cuadrada,* best translated as *blockhead.* Hoover not only fit the description, he flaunted it with a severe Marine-style crew cut. His dark eyebrows spread across the bridge of his nose, but he didn't trim or pluck them; he seemed to cultivate the image of a Stone-Age brute. It was his form of charm, a rough man's version of my mother's philosophy: if God gives you lemons, make lemonade.

While Hoover enumerated his daughter's many talents, Beto returned with a music stand and a stool, as well as the flute and an assortment of sheet music. Magdalena dutifully put together the flute. I wondered how often she and her father had performed this ritual of coax and protest. I wondered how reluctant she was to play.

A drop of sweat slid down the inside of my armpit. The heat of the afternoon had collected in the room, despite the high ceiling and open windows. I should have been cool in my ridiculous outfit, but I was nervous for Magdalena.

"This is a duet for guitar and flute," she said. "The guitar is missing."

She arched her back and raised the flute to her lips. The first notes wavered just off pitch, a shaky, hollow sound that gradually gained fullness of tone as her eyelids drooped lower and lower.

Only her mother kept talking. She giggled into Spoon's ear and waltzed him over to me. "I'm Connie," she said. "I love your shirt." She offered her hand, and out of panic I kissed it. "You're as bad as Patricio," she said, brushing her rose against my cheek before she cruised back to the kitchen.

My involvement with classical music ended in tenth grade, when, like any red-blooded American boy, I chose second-string right fielder over first-chair viola. Believe it or not, I missed the tedious rehearsals and the moody orchestra conductor. But what I really missed was the music, its power to convey pure emotion. Magdalena's piece conveyed desire. She played with great restraint, holding each low note a little longer than necessary. As the melody rose to a higher register, her right foot, in its subversive purple sneaker, tapped faster.

Hoover glanced at his watch, at the front door, at the guests ringing the room. Spoon's wide grin slowly narrowed into a more sober expression. I felt keenly aware of every nuance in the music and every distraction.

Magdalena held herself apart from the growing passion of the one-sided duet. She filled each note with denial. Her stiff posture, her resolute stillness reminded me of the way she'd walked with Spoon—arm in arm, but distant. She didn't bend to the music. She achieved a purity of tone that Sonny by the fire in the Mission had never approached, but he'd let the music escape him raw, whereas she worked it in her mind into something more cerebral, less basic. I wondered how she'd resolve the conflict between the movement of the piece toward an ecstatic climax and her own unyielding resistance.

I never found out. A powerful motorcycle roared up to the front door, a motorcycle in dire need of a new muffler. The engine revved several times, rattling the champagne bottles in the buckets of ice.

Magdalena shut her mouth. Her narrow shoulders shook. I don't know if she was too far outside herself or too far in, but when Spoon knelt beside her, she put down her flute, summoned a semblance of composure, and fled.

The man who'd ruined her performance embraced Hoover in a powerful bear hug. I felt almost proper compared to this intruder, who wore black combat boots, camouflage fatigues, a leather vest, and no shirt. No hair, either. His head was shaved, maybe even oiled. It glistened like an egg fried in too much butter.

"Mouseketeers, meet Marlón," Spoon said. "My future *cuñado.*"

Cuñado is Spanish for brother-in-law. Spanish has a special set of words for in-laws and God-relatives and the other important relations in a person's life. This important relation scratched his chest as he headed straight for Spoon and me. Reaching out as if to shake Spoon's hand, he snagged a bottle of champagne instead. As if in response to a challenge, Spoon popped open another bottle, held it up at arm's length, and let the champagne cascade into his mouth. Marlón imitated the technique. It was what we called in Reedley a chugalug contest.

The colonel in the wheelchair clapped his hands and chanted "*Vi-no, vi-no.*" His wife and a few others joined in.

Spoon nonchalantly pretended to yawn, as if he could go on drinking forever.

Marlón stomped his combat boot near Spoon's exposed toes. If he missed on purpose, he cut it close. He reminded me of men at Lorna's health spa who admired their own flexed biceps from as many angles as possible.

His bottle emptied less quickly than Spoon's. Spoon opened his throat so that the champagne poured down. Marlón swallowed. His Adam's apple bobbed. Champagne collected in his mouth, trickled down each side of his chin. With his free hand, Spoon groped in the ice bucket for another bottle, which he thrust in my direction. "Enough," I said, but I uncorked it for him. He smoothly made the switch. I uncorked a second bottle for Marlón because it seemed like the fair thing to do, but Marlón swallowed wrong and coughed up a throatful of champagne. Spoon pounded him on the back much harder than necessary until Hoover stepped between them like a referee stopping a fight.

"Ladies and gentlemen," Hoover said. "Monsignor Spigarelli. Now that my entire family is assembled, I must issue an important proclamation. You all know that I am losing my lovely daughter to this fine Dr. Patricio McGuffin. You may not know that Dr. McGuffin is a licensed anthropologist from the University of California. Years ago he came to me with a letter of introduction from his illustrious father, a magnificent patriot who once performed great service for the freedom of our country.

"I provided what assistance I could for don Patricio. I introduced him to my coffee workers, and he saw fit to spend time with them, to study the quaint ways of our indigenous people.

"Last month, when his research was finally completed—it will be available soon in libraries and bookstores—he came to me again to ask a second favor. He'd hardly set foot in this house since the first visit, despite the enticement of the most beautiful girl in Guatemala, but I listened to his request. Would I sponsor a little election among my workers? All would benefit, don Patricio insisted. Improved conditions would improve production. He appealed to me both as a businessman and as a humanitarian.

"Well, I promised to think the matter over. *Yanquis* don't have all the answers, but I gave the matter serious thought. And then, as suddenly as the crickets take to chirping before an earthquake, don Patricio and Magdalena fell in love. I decided that I should be honored to have a son-in-law who wished to improve the business of the family. In short, I am pleased to announce that this coming Thursday we will hold a little election at La Esperanza, overseen by Dr. Patricio McGuffin, security provided by Lieutenant Marlón de Montenegro Schultz, my renegade Apache of a son, and perhaps our new friend, Señor Armando Santiesteban, a *Harvard man,* will ensure the full legality of the proceedings. In fact, if don Patricio's father arrives by Thursday, he too can lend a hand to this little exercise in democracy."

Throughout his flowery speech Hoover kept a firm grip on Marlón and Spoon. With his free hand, Marlón tossed pieces of ice in the air and caught most of them in his mouth. Spoon made a show of drinking more champagne.

The mention of his father brought his drinking to a stop. He rapped his bottle against the edge of the table to get everyone's attention. "I'm very sorry to have to tell you that my father will not be here. He suffered a serious heart attack and lacks the strength to travel. Naturally, my mother will be staying with him. But they wish to invite—"

"Nonsense," Hoover said. "Your father is indestructible. I'll have Beto put through a call."

Marlón pried Hoover's fingers one by one from his wrist. Hoover grabbed him by the vest, but he simply shrugged out of it.

"I'm busy Thursday," he said.

"Then rearrange your schedule," Hoover said.

If Marlón was named after Brando, he certainly lived up to the swaggering slouch, the malicious, almost feminine sneer. His lips were thinner than Brando's, but he had the same kind of pampered face. Maybe his mother had loved *The Wild One* or *On the Waterfront*. Or maybe she'd just wanted to name her son after an American movie star. He pinched one of the few hairs on his bare chest and idly plucked it out.

"I'd appreciate your help with this election," Spoon said. He offered Marlón his hand again, and this time Marlón shook it.

"Blessed are the peacemakers," the monsignor said.

Marlón's slack smile didn't waver, but his grip visibly tightened. The guests at a distance probably saw a warm display of friendship, but I saw Spoon's knees dip inward. His jaw clenched and his forehead broke a sweat. Hoover, after a moment's hesitation, took hold of the back of Marlón's thick neck and squeezed. Magdalena's mother, Connie, hurried over from the kitchen doorway and pinched Marlón's arm. When that didn't work, she made him lean sideways to hear a secret and then planted her tongue in his ear. Marlón bolted upright and let go of Spoon, who flexed his bloodshot hand as indifferently as he could.

"Let's have a photograph to commemorate this inspired collaboration," Hoover said.

"I'd better go check on Magdalena," Spoon said.

"A little moment," Hoover said, snapping his fingers. A bespectacled photographer stepped forward and nervously popped in a new flashbulb.

"I won't have your election interfere with my wedding," Magdalena's mother said.

"Of course not, my beloved Connie," Hoover said. "But what greater assistance could I provide than to keep these difficult men out of your hair until Friday?"

While the photographer spread a white handkerchief under his knee, Hoover shooed his beloved Connie out of the picture. When she didn't move fast enough, he snatched up her rose and pelted her with it, not a vicious blow, but not a playful love tap either. He hooked his arms around Marlón and Spoon, both of whom towered over him. The photographer asked them to say *thirty-three*—the Guatemalan equivalent of *cheese*—but Hoover imperiously snapped his fingers again, this time for Magdalena's stool, which was fetched to boost him to the height he deserved. The flash of the flashbulb caught his brief, triumphant smile. I thought of that smile later in the privacy of my upstairs bedroom as I unpacked, ironed my suit, and waited for Spoon. I couldn't get it out of my mind, the diabolical pleasure with which Hoover had posed on that stool, as if he'd fooled Mother Nature, as if he'd put one over on God Himself.

V

TRAVEL IN STYLE

We all live by robbing . . . coolies, and those of us who are enlightened all maintain that those coolies ought to be set free; but our standard of living, and hence our enlightenment, demands that the robbery shall continue.

GEORGE ORWELL

My mother used to call me a camel of sleep. When I was a kid and my father was out of town hauling peaches or nectarines to Riverside or San Bernardino, she'd let me sleep late into the afternoon, later than any of my friends, not only because she knew how much I loved to sleep, but also because my father when he was home always woke me up so unreasonably early to do what we called fruit work—picking, sorting, packing, labeling. My mother didn't want me to resent my father. She claimed that I could store sleep for the times I needed it most.

I loved to sleep. And I loved to wake up slowly. Spoon deprived me of both those pleasures when he tickled my feet and started whistling the theme from "The Bridge Over the River Kwai."

"All aboard for La Esperanza!" he said with malicious enthusiasm.

I muttered vague syllables of discontent. The bedside light was still on. The book I'd been reading poked into my ribs.

"Rise and shine. Hup hup hup. Seize the day."

"What happened last night? Where were you?"

"Placating Magdalena. She copped a mood. But she got over it."

"I waited up for you," I said. I couldn't keep from whining. The sky outside the oval window was suspiciously black.

"Management sincerely regrets any inconvenience."

"I don't mind being left alone, but I'd appreciate a word of explanation."

Spoon rubbed his knuckles against his cheek and I noticed
that it was smooth, baby smooth. He'd shaved his scruffy beard
and looked less sardonic than usual, less impervious. They say
that the eyes are the windows of the soul, but what gave Spoon
away was his mouth. His naked mouth seemed to reveal even
the most infinitesimal flickerings of doubt and fear.

"Magdalena needed some TLC. She doesn't have complete
faith in me yet. I think I reassured her."

He peered at the neat arrangement of my things on the oak
desk. For a second I suspected he might sweep them onto the
floor, but he just picked up the canister of mace my mother had
given me for my birthday and pressed the plunger lightly
enough to test its resistance.

"I wish we could have tried a little sexual healing. The room
they put me in has the squeakiest bed. It goes off like a burglar
alarm if you so much as breathe heavy."

I wanted to blast him for deserting me. I wanted to demand
an apology for his deceitful remark at the reception. *Armando
works for one of the most esteemed law firms in San Francisco.* He'd
led everyone to believe that I was an attorney—as if a lowly
word processor weren't good enough for him. Now I wanted to
hurt him back, but he seemed so unprotected. The stillness of
the hour amplified his deep, despondent breath.

"You okay?" I said.

He whirled around and aimed the mace right between
my eyes. I wouldn't have been too surprised if he'd sprayed me
with it.

"What's the plan?" I said. "Just give me a rough idea."

"Hoover's grand tour of the coffee plantation. A visit to my
friends at the lake. Maybe even a steam bath in an authentic
Indian sweat lodge."

"Should I bring Sonny's package?"

"We may have to drop it in the mail. This election won't
leave us much time. But bring it along. And don't forget the
mace—although I think your handy travel iron might be a
deadlier weapon." He yanked the covers off my bed. "Everybody out for volleyball. Happy days are here again."

The strain in his voice made me wonder which of us he was trying to convince.

My knees bounced against Spoon's in the back of Hoover's Land Rover while the sun rose west of Guatemala City on Highway 2. It was the second most spellbinding dawn I've ever seen. Trees carved themselves out of the dark. A gray woman encouraged a gray mule up a roadside gully with vigorous hatslaps to the flanks. Stars blinked out as the sky turned a shallower and shallower blue.

Hoover disrupted the spell when he swung around in the shotgun seat and resumed the argument he and Spoon had begun at breakfast.

"Peasants aren't forced at gunpoint to buy Coca-Cola," Hoover said, unzipping a pocket of his safari vest and extracting a cigar.

"That doesn't mean the choice is free," Spoon said. "A whole new culture has been imposed without respect for their beliefs."

The Land Rover swerved around a dead owl. Hoover's servant Beto drove as if he were paid a bonus for every movement of the steering wheel.

"I'll tell you about beliefs," Hoover said. "Beliefs mean nothing to a bullet. We could be fired on by guerrillas right now, and the bullets might miss the capitalist pig and hit the peasant"—he fisted Beto in the shoulder—"or the Communist sympathizer, or even the innocent bystander. So note well which side you're on. When the bullets fly, you're the enemy, regardless of your beliefs."

"I'm aware of that irony," Spoon said. Watching a green-and-orange bird peck a worm from a puddle of mud, I tried to hang on to the magic of the sunrise, but Spoon raised his voice so high over the throb of the Land Rover that I couldn't shut him out. "It's a shame we're so clearly identified as the cause of all the problems. But it's our own fault. The United States has supported business and profits instead of freedom and human rights. That's our downfall. That's our fatal flaw."

"You're crazy," Hoover said. "Is that not true, Armando?" I nodded attentively. "Patricio wasn't here when the big earthquake struck in 1976, but the United States, our greatest friend, provided not only doctors but also food and medical supplies and material for the reconstruction of houses."

"But who got it?" Spoon said. "I've interviewed Refugio and Hércules and dozens of others. I know what happened in the villages. Politicians, from the President down to the most petty *alcalde*, peddled that stuff for profit or gave it away to their henchmen. The United States supported the power structure, not the people."

"What twisted, demented rhetoric!" Hoover said. "And typical of the guerilla mentality, I must observe. No matter how much kindness one does for the peasants, their complaints become more bitter and resentful."

Spoon rocked back and forth in the throes of debate frenzy. "Suppose I stood over you with my boot grinding into your neck. Suppose I had been standing over you like that for five hundred years. If I decided to take a little pressure off, if I removed the boot entirely, would you say thank you? Would you consider it an act of kindness and be grateful?"

Hoover puffed his cigar till the tip glowed. "Your words are the words of an outsider, full of abstract theory but devoid of experience. I envy your enthusiasm, but you don't understand the give and take of our system, our generous compromises. *I keep a thousand families alive.* Without the landowners, without men of ambitious vision, there would be no Guatemala, just primitive tribes, amusing for North American anthropologists, no doubt, but useless for anything else."

The argument wore on. The Land Rover filled with cigar smoke. The sun beat down on the back of my neck and the colors of the landscape flattened. Dawn was far behind us now, but there had been a moment when I imagined a mule and then saw it. If I had imagined a zebra, I might have seen one. That's how full of wonder the world at dawn had seemed. Not at this hour, though. Not with the sun bleaching everything in sight. Now I had to admit that the world remained the same from moment to moment. Mules remained mules. Shacks remained shacks. I felt sick to my stomach. The slow bus in front of us belched a cloud of black smoke.

We remained stuck behind that bus all the way up to the military checkpoint at the top of the pass. A row of six oil drums blocked traffic in both directions. Skinny soldiers strutted around like rock stars. Hoover reached across Beto and honked the horn. The nearest soldier checked his bullet clip, wiped his nose, and swaggered over.

I expected him to be bigger and older, but up close he barely stood tall enough to set his whiskerless chin on Beto's half-lowered window. He had an oddly shaped skull, larger on the left side than the right, a runny nose, and a mean, frightened mouth. He was just a boy, even younger than my brother Bobby, just a boy with a loaded weapon that banged against the door of the Land Rover as he reached in and demanded our papers.

"I want Lieutenant Rodríguez!" Hoover barked.

The soldier tensed. "Yes, sir," he said, squinting over the edge of the window at Hoover. "On the part of whom, sir?"

Hoover passed him a laminated white card and warned him not to get his dirty fingerprints on it. The soldier saluted semi-respectfully and marched up the hillside toward a cluster of tents.

Meanwhile, all the men and boys had stepped down from the bus in front of us. There were four Americans among them, four unmistakable party animals in plaid shorts and identical yellow tank tops that said "I Survived Hussong's Cantina." They punched each other, laughed, and played catch with their passports while one of the soldiers worked his way down the line, checking each identity card, even the driver's, until he came to a small boy no more than twelve years old. He put his hand on the boy's head and guided him out of the line.

A much bigger boy began to cry. The soldier hadn't reached him yet, but the big boy's chest heaved, tears ran down his pudgy cheeks, he bit his fist.

An old woman leaned out a window of the bus and pleaded with the soldier. "Leave Miguelito. I need Miguelito. His mother lies sick with bad intestines. We bring special herbs to cure the bad. Please, sir. The boy goes to join the army in less than a month. Let him visit his sick mother with me."

The soldier shrugged. "If he's joining in a month, he might as well join now."

The big boy ran to his grandmother's window and jumped, as if she could catch him in her arms and squeeze him through the window to safety.

The smaller boy stood quietly with his hands behind his back. If he had a mother or sister or grandmother on the bus, she kept just as quiet as he did.

The party animals stopped monkeying around. They handed over their passports without a wisecrack. A wind blew through the oak trees. The big boy's sobbing seemed to grow louder and louder.

"What do you think of the Guatemalan draft?" Spoon asked me. "The army is an equal opportunity abductor."

"Most are eager to serve their country," Hoover said.

The lieutenant knocked on our windshield then. He was a sharp-featured young man with a flamboyant handlebar mustache that he must have tended with great care during the tedious hours in his tent. His gold fillings glinted when he spoke. "Always an honor, don Hoover," he said.

They inquired about each other's family, Hoover contributed the contents of a sealed envelope to a fund for *viudas y huérfanos* (yes, widows and orphans, that's right), and the lieutenant ordered his chastened private to treat us with the utmost courtesy on all our journeys this way.

As we wheeled around the smog-chuffing bus, I caught a glimpse of the two boys being led up the hill. They trudged past a long banner stretched between drooping oaks. It proclaimed in red letters: "Home of the Fighting Jaguars, Proudest Corps in Guatemala."

There's a Guatemalan expression I learned from Spoon: "*El café es brujo*"—coffee is a sorcerer. I can't imagine an expression like that about peaches or nectarines. In the San Joaquin Valley, the fields are discrete, the rows regular, the trees uniform. The land is *under cultivation;* man has the upper hand. I remember riding home in the back of an open truck at the end of a long workday the summer before college, craning my neck to catch the faint spray of irrigation water. I hated the heat and the itchy peach fuzz, but I appreciated the design, the beauty of agriculture.

I missed that reassuring order at La Esperanza. The deep green of the coffee trees vibrated with supernatural intensity. There were no right angles, no flat fields, just a jumble of steep hills, corrugated metal shacks, and a run-down hacienda.

The noontime hush surrounded us when the Land Rover stopped. A ribbon of dust had risen over the rutted, unpaved road; it resettled exceedingly slowly. Late April is the end of the dry season in Guatemala, the middle of the off-season for coffee. A group of twenty or thirty men worked on the hill sloping down to the hacienda. Some mended branches trampled or bent during harvest. Others trimmed the tall banana trees planted at the end of each ragged row. Their white shirts flashed amid the green. The blades of their machetes glinted in the dull sunshine.

The best thing about the hacienda was the immense bola tree out front. The worst thing was the stuffed alligator head mounted over the floor safe in the office. Whether as a joke or a warning, the plastic arm of a mannequin protruded from the alligator's mouth. Hoover showed more interest in the safe itself, a squat steel vault that he claimed could withstand an explosion of up to twenty-five sticks of dynamite. His foreman grunted to confirm the fact.

The foreman was a dour, chinless man named Benigno. He had his houseboy fetch us warm Coca-Colas but didn't drink one himself. He followed at a deferential distance when we tromped out back to look at what Hoover called "the heart of the operation"—concrete drying platforms, a set of scales, washing tanks, an ancient gasoline-powered hulling machine, and dozens of dilapidated storage sheds. La Esperanza was not a state-of-the-art coffee plantation.

By the time we finished our tour, Beto had laid out a picnic under the bola tree. The houseboy brought Hoover a rocking chair. Spoon and I shared a log. Beto filled our plates with leftovers from the reception.

"One day this could all be yours," Hoover said to Spoon with no detectable irony.

"I'd give it back to the *campesinos*," Spoon said.

"Don't be ridiculous," Hoover said. "It was never theirs." He devoured a hunk of goat cheese and went on. "Indians lack the coffee mentality. New shrubs take four years to bear."

"Indians don't have patience?" Spoon said.

"Indians don't have foresight," Hoover said. "They don't have cunning. One can't run a big operation without cunning."

"Then let them learn," Spoon said. "As far as I'm concerned, the biggest problem in Guatemala is the distribution of land. Two percent of the landowners control seventy percent of the land. That's criminal. And besides, it's a ticket to disaster."

"Be practical, Patricio, please. If you gave this land to the peasants, they'd sell it at the next fiesta. They'd get twice as drunk for a few weeks. You see? Some other shrewd investor would acquire it all, only he might not be as civilized as you or I. Understand me?"

Spoon spread duck liver pâté on a cracker. "We're talking strictly in the abstract?" he asked.

"Marlón will never care about this place. It doesn't make enough noise. You know how to touch people. You have a light hand."

"Thank you," Spoon said. "Believe me, I appreciate your efforts on behalf of the workers. Not all the *fincas* pay as well. But even here at La Esperanza, a hundred twenty pounds of coffee are weighed as a hundred."

"Our scales don't lie!" Hoover insisted as he bit into an overflowing mushroom.

"I've heard that if the scale-master finds a single green berry among the ripe ones, a dollar is subtracted. If the worker is accused of damaging a single tree, a dollar is subtracted. Instead of three dollars and twenty-five cents a day, the worker earns a dollar. For brutal work."

"Oh, now, picking coffee is not so brutal. You go at your own pace, in the shade of the banana trees —"

"Bent low in extreme heat, you pick as fast as you can, slap the bugs, wipe the sweat away, and then, if you don't get sick from the insecticide or the tainted water, you live on nothing but beans and tortillas till you return to your village. That's brutal work."

"It's honorable work which must be done. The Indians, thank God, are well adapted to it. They don't suffer the way we would, we creatures of luxury. They're tough, they don't expect much, they accept the world as it is. Truly, Patricio, they resist change on principle. You overlook that crucial fact."

The men on the hillside had worked their way across to the crooked road. Two women walked up from the shacks with flat straw baskets and a cast-iron bucket trailing steam. The men in the banana trees climbed down, stuck their machetes in the ground, and rolled cigarettes or drank water from a goatskin.

Hoover slipped two fingers in his mouth and whistled. One of the men tugged his canvas hat in polite acknowledgment. Hoover waved him in our direction. The man came trotting down the hill.

"Pay attention," Hoover said. "Learn from this experiment."

The man stopped short of our circle of shade, took off his hat, and bowed toward each of us.

"Tomás, my good friend, grab a plate and eat," Hoover said.

"You are very kind, *patrón.*"

"*Approveche.*" Dig in.

Tomás bowed again, but remained in the sun. Beto made no move to serve him as he'd served us.

"Please," Hoover said. "Help yourself."

As if he were entering a mine field, Tomás stepped up to the blanket on which lay Tupperware containers and a silver tray. After much deliberation, he glanced at his dirty hands, wavered over the chicken wings and the cakes, then selected one sesame seed cracker, which he ate in small bites, smiling as he chewed.

"Very flavorful," he said when he finished. "And crisp."

The foreman watched us from the porch, idly snapping and unsnapping the flap of the black holster he wore on his hip. The men on the hillside took their food from the women. The women didn't eat.

"Tomás has a very good hand with coffee," Hoover said. "And no one prunes the shade trees better. It's a delicate operation. Young coffee needs more shade. In higher altitudes, less. When the soil is deeper and richer, you have to account for that. Tomás is an artist. Years ago he taught me the secrets of sun and shade. And now he's a candidate to lead the workers. I'm sure he'll do a fine job."

"Whatever you think best, *patrón*, but I am very old," Tomás said. "I know a little about coffee, but I know very little about men."

"Try a mushroom," Hoover said.

"No thank you, sir, if it's all the same to you. My poor blood is much too thin."

"You see?" Hoover said to Spoon. "This is what would happen to your grand reforms. *No thank you, sir. You're much too kind.* A few might nibble your exotic mushroom, but none would swallow. If you wish to bring progress to La Esperanza, you must change the diet bean by bean."

"I could never run this farm," Spoon said with his winning boyish grin. "And you don't expect me to."

"Why not? Engels ran a factory and supported Marx with the profits. Certainly *you* could adjust to such a contradiction."

Spoon waved his hand at the hillside, our lunch, the hacienda. "No matter how enlightened you are or I am, this is exploitation. I wouldn't want to be part of that."

The creases along Hoover's forehead deepened; his thick black eyebrows bunched together over the bridge of his nose. "I find your attitude indefensible," he said.

Spoon gnawed his chicken wing down to the bone, licked his long fingers, and wiped them against the soft satin napkin on his knee. "Believe me, don Hoover, I appreciate the difficult realities of your position. I know it's hard to keep your hands clean in a dirty world. But—"

"But nothing! You imply that your hands are cleaner than mine. We have a saying in the Schultz family. *He who sleeps in the guest room sleeps in the house.*"

"I agree. Directly or indirectly, we all benefit from the dirty work others do. *We*, meaning those of us—"

"Excuse me," Hoover said. "Let's be perfectly honest here. We both know your father pockets thirty-five percent of the profits of La Esperanza. How can you call that indirect?"

Spoon's plate teetered on his lap. "I believe the bulk of my father's money comes from my mother's tobacco stock."

"Perhaps so, perhaps not. But my accountant has mailed him a check every three months for nearly thirty years. Believe me, he's never failed to cash it."

Spoon set his plate down on the ground. He lowered his head so far his chin touched his collarbone. He looked as if the life spark had gone out of him. "If what you say is true," he said softly, "I'll pay back my share. Little by little. I never asked *him* for that money and I never asked *you*. So don't accuse me of exploiting these people."

"Patricio, Patricio, no one's accusing you. We're not enemies. I'm glad you've benefitted from our profits. Do you boys want this cake?"

"No," Spoon said. "No thank you."

"Tomás, why don't you run some cake up to your people there? Take the mushrooms if you want."

Tomás carefully stacked a dozen cakes in the crown of his hat, bowed in thanks, and trotted up the hill.

"Now," Hoover said. "About this election. One piece of advice. Your friend Hércules attracts a certain element we don't need around here. His participation should be discouraged."

Spoon sprang to his feet. "Is that an order?"

"Let's discuss practical matters," Hoover said. "You'll need ballots. A voting booth, perhaps. All the resident workers will vote, of course, and whatever seasonal workers show up with pay stubs."

"Wait," Spoon said. "I don't feel comfortable with your demand. My policy as an anthropologist is noninterference."

"*La puta mierda!*" Hoover said. "Your mere presence is interference."

"I observe and ask questions. That's all."

"Don't pretend to underestimate your own significance. You've fed these Indians plenty of new ideas."

"They've fed me."

Hoover began to rock. "Listen, my son. You and I are embarking on a lifelong voyage. Why not use your influence for the good of everyone?"

Spoon rubbed his knuckles where his beard had been. "The irony is that Hércules would never run for anything unless someone told him he couldn't. Don't you see that? It's such a waste."

"You pushed for this election," Hoover said.

"I know. And now I feel like I can't participate."

"We've had radio announcements in Sololá and Quezaltenango." Hoover brought the rocking chair to a stop. "I did everything I could to promote your studies."

"You have my gratitude."

"But not your respect? It's important that we treat each other with consideration."

"What if I promised not to encourage Hércules? Would that satisfy you?"

"Let's not bicker any longer," Hoover said. "Help me up. My bones are heavy. Beto, feed those mushrooms to the goats."

Spoon gave Hoover a halfhearted tug. The foreman discreetly presented himself for instructions.

"My son-in-law and his *compadre* will be staying a few nights," Hoover said. "Help them arrange for the election on Thursday. Have you found a second candidate yet?"

The foreman cast a tentative glance at his houseboy, who was already hauling the rocking chair back to the porch.

"Perhaps other candidates will step forward," Hoover said. "The important thing is to have at least two."

"Excuse me, don Hoover," Spoon said. "I thought Armando and I might visit Lake Atitlán this afternoon. I want him to meet my friends."

"As you wish," Hoover said. He ordered the foreman to bring around the Chevy for us.

"Oh, no," Spoon said. "That won't be necessary. Armando and I can walk to Cuatro Caminos and catch a bus from there. It's a chance for him to experience the native way of life."

"Armando," Hoover said. "You've been so quiet. What's your impression of La Esperanza?"

"It's beautiful," I said.

"You must see these hills in late October, when the white flowers bloom. Exquisite. Heartbreaking. Isn't there anything you boys will let me do for you?"

I'd stopped eating during the argument and now the yellow cornmeal cakes looked particularly good, but Spoon seemed determined to refuse all offers, at least for the moment.

We said our good-byes and grabbed our gear from the Land Rover. Spoon hoisted his duffel over his shoulder and led the way up the hill toward Tomás and his men. They'd gone back to work, two to a row, patiently bracing the damaged limbs of the coffee shrubs. Tomás himself had climbed one of the tall banana trees next to the road. With his legs wrapped around a swaying branch, he waved his machete and called down to us: "Many thanks for the gift of cakes."

I tried dragging my Samsonite, but the road had too many bumps. Spoon set a stiff pace, leaning into the heat as if he could slice through it. My gray Hush Puppies turned brown with dust. The sound of our breathing grew so loud I didn't hear the Land Rover until it rolled by us, stopping a dozen yards ahead and backing up.

"Cuatro Caminos?" Hoover said.

"It's not that much farther," Spoon said.

"So why not travel in style?" Hoover said.

Spoon wiped his face with his shirtsleeve. My sleeves were much too sweaty for that to work.

"Why not travel in style?" Spoon said to me. "The ultimate question of conscience."

His sunglasses slipped down his nose. For just an instant I saw him as an old professor, stooped and cynical, disgusted by his own conclusions.

"It's a black day in Dallas," he said.

We climbed in.

VI

HERCULES AND REFUGIO

As for their carriage and behavior, the Indians are very courteous and loving, and of timorous nature, and willing to serve and obey, and to be good, if they be drawn by love; but when they are too much tyrannized, they are dogged, unwilling to please, or to work, and will choose rather strangling and death than life.

THOMAS GAGE

Our freshman year of college, I found Spoon sitting alone in our dorm room one dismal November afternoon with the shades lowered and the lights off. I hung up my raincoat and umbrella. Spoon didn't move. He had his elbows on his desk, shoulders hunched forward, both thumbs shoved deep into his mouth. He was crying—or almost crying. Tears ran down his cheeks, but no sound escaped him.

I sat down at my desk, put my feet up, and waited. I'd only known Spoon a few months, but already I'd decided that he was the most relentlessly upbeat person I'd ever met. After a long time, he took his thumbs out of his mouth, looked up at me, and said, "It's a black day in Dallas." Then he looked down again.

I couldn't tell if he was looking at anything in particular. It was November 22, an anniversary of the Kennedy assassination, but I couldn't imagine Spoon mourning a President. His breathing gradually evened out. The rain fell on the leaves of the trees outside our window. The radiator knocked. After another long silence, he grabbed his reading lamp and smashed it so hard against his desk that the bulb shattered. Then he picked up a small fragment of the bulb, placed it on his tongue like a holy wafer, and chewed.

I went over to him; swept the pieces of the light bulb into the wastebasket. His wallet, I noticed before he snapped it shut, lay open to a picture of his little sister. After that, on those rare occasions when the dark mood caught him, he'd say, "It's a black day in Dallas," and I'd leave him alone, but I'd keep an eye on him.

His sister died toward the end of 1963. I hadn't heard the whole story, even though he usually told me everything. He told everybody everything. Once at a Taco Bell, he casually confided to several of our dorm-mates that he'd dreamed of having sex with me in the boiler room of a steamship. There were only two subjects he avoided: his trust fund and his sister. On those subjects he brooded.

So I let him brood. I read my paperback while we waited at Cuatro Caminos, which consisted of two gas pumps, a storefront, and an occasional passing truck. I watched the curious interplay of children, chickens, and a baby pig during the dusty bus ride to Patulul, where they served the sweetest Fanta Orange in the world. Spoon drank his without a word, and I didn't press him. I assumed that his brooding would follow its typical volcanic pattern—dormant phase, eruption—but on the bus to Santiago Atitlán something out of the ordinary happened.

We traveled the Prince of Peace line. Three crucifixes hung from the rearview mirror. A bloodcurdling poster of Christ was taped to the back of the driver's seat. Twice the bus sped past people who obviously wanted a ride. Once it stopped for several minutes in an absolutely deserted place where no one got off or on.

We balanced in the crowded aisle next to three heavyset Ladino women who avidly discussed Spoon's physique in Spanish. They called him a long red chili pepper, they called him a pineapple head, they called him words I'd never heard before. "Look at the faces he makes," they said.

It was true. Spoon scowled, grimaced, frowned, squinted, pursed his lips, gritted his teeth, rolled his eyes, sighed, stared up at the rust-scarred ceiling. The Ladino women seemed to suffer with him.

Then one of them began to sing. She had warts on her neck, pitted skin, and a narrow, crooked nose, but her voice, even over the dreary engine whine, emerged strong and clear. She sang without shyness or theatricality, as if she were simply letting the song loose:

> *Jesus gives me freedom*
> *Freedom*
> *Freedom*
> *Jesus gives me freedom*
> *No one will ever take from me.*

> *There is no sadness*
> *No hardship*
> *No oppression*
> *Only freedom.*

> *Jesus gives me freedom*
> *Freedom*
> *Freedom*
> *Jesus gives me freedom*
> *No one will ever take from me.*

Spoon didn't look near her at first, but his face unscrunched and the tight wrinkles around his eyes gradually faded. He dug into his duffel for a Mickey Mouse balloon, blew it up, and batted it toward the back of the bus. The balloon was passed around almost reverently. People sniffed, listened, shook. When it popped in the hands of a muckle-mouthed girl, everyone laughed, and that was as close to an eruption as Spoon got.

For the rest of the ride, he talked to me in English. He said that Spanish would embarrass the women who had been gossiping about him. He didn't bring up the trust fund. Instead, he told the story of Hércules and Refugio.

Hércules Gavilán had entered the world coughing. When the coughing turned into rheumatic fever, his mother brought him to the young priest in Santiago Atitlán. The priest arranged for treatment at a hospital in the capital, but Hércules remained scrawny and sickly. He could never catch his breath and his eyes watered. The priest liked him, though. He became the priest's pet project. He learned to read and write and assist the priest with holy rituals.

One day, when Hércules was seven or eight, the priest found him behind the church throwing knives at a cypress tree. All three knives stuck in the same spot.

"You're going to get in trouble with those knives," the priest told him.

"No, Father," he answered very seriously. "I'm going to get in trouble without them."

At twelve or thirteen, he began to put on weight. His family took him back. He went to work on the coast with his father and brothers. Within a few years, a local businessman named Pepe Bustamante rewarded his diligence and good Spanish. Don Pepe received a commission for every crew he sent to the coffee plantations. He made Hércules a crew chief, then a driver, and then Hércules decided that don Pepe pocketed too big a share of the workers' wages. Hércules borrowed money from the priest who'd raised him and bought a truck of his own. He went into competition with don Pepe and eventually did well, because he was honest and people respected him and he accepted less of a commission.

Soon one of the men from his parents' village approached him about joining a cooperative. The man wanted him to take local textile goods to Guatemala City and bring back supplies for the cooperative store. This man was Refugio Díaz, Spoon's principal informant. Spoon often stayed at Refugio's house and rode in the truck with Hércules. Thanks mainly to the two of them, the cooperative had built a mill to grind corn and an oven to bake bread, its store was breaking even, and its textile business occasionally showed a small profit.

"I owe my Ph.D. to these guys," Spoon said. "They really showed me the world of the seasonal workers. And they did what only your very best friends can do—they taught me something about how to live. I hope you feel it. They're true heroes of our time."

A dented Studebaker Champ bounced us down the narrow, winding road to San Blás del Lago, the Ladino town next to Santa Catalina del Lago, which was Indian. "The unwanted Indian stepchild," Spoon called it. He explained that the two

towns regularly disputed boundaries, water rights, and government aid, and that Santa Catalina lost every time. The
pavement, for instance, ran out just past San Blás.

Spoon stopped our taxi driver at the edge of the pavement.

"Rocks—no problem," the driver said.

"We'll walk," Spoon said.

"We will?" I said.

"Solidarity with the *campesinos*," Spoon said. I couldn't decide if he was joking or not.

And so we entered Santa Catalina on foot. The sun had
dropped below the ridge of mountains to our west, but the air
was still warm and the pale light was thrilling.

A gaggle of small boys surrounded us within seconds. They
wrestled for the privilege of carrying Spoon's bag. A few of the
losers settled for my Samsonite. Spoon rewarded all of them,
doling out bubble gum, sticks of red licorice, and more balloons.

There were no words on the sign outside the cooperative
store, just a carved picture of an ear of corn. Inside, a small man
sat bent over a wooden table, methodically penciling an entry
into his ledger. He was fiftyish, frail-looking, with thinning hair,
a drooping mouth, and heavy black Buddy Holly glasses. The
thick lenses made his large eyes seem even larger. They glistened, as if swollen with tears, but his expression when he
looked up was full of joy.

"My book?" he said, touching fingertips with Spoon.

"Not yet," Spoon said. "But I guarantee you an autographed
edition as soon as it's published."

"Ah, but will you translate it into Spanish for me?"

"Of course not. I don't want you to read my lies."

Instead of shaking my hand, Refugio touched my fingertips.
It was a regional custom, but I'll always associate it with
Refugio because it suited him so well: gentle, gracious, hinting
of magic.

"You must wield quite an influence with Señor McGuffin,"
he said. "I've never seen his entire face before."

Spoon stroked his naked cheeks. "I'm joining the establishment," he said. "The heart of the oligarchy. Don Hoover's daughter accepted my proposal."

"May God bless your union with heavenly light," Refugio said. He whistled like a bird and a skinny teenage boy crawled out from behind the counter. "Run get Hércules and tell your mother to borrow a chicken from María Cruz."

"The wedding is Saturday," Spoon said. "I need you to be there."

"Of course, of course," Refugio said.

A woman appeared in the doorway, blocking what little light filtered into the store. She was terrifyingly skinny. Her spidery hands trembled as she unfolded four very small green shirts and smoothed them out on the table. I couldn't help staring at her brittle wrists, no thicker than my thumbs.

Refugio spoke to her in a language of guttural consonants and sharp vowels. Her head drooped lower and lower.

"She doesn't understand how big *yanquis* are," Refugio said. "Big. See?" He had Spoon stand up to emphasize the point. He held a small shirt to Spoon's chest.

Her expression remained impassive. Refugio slipped her a handful of coins and let her keep the shirts. It was only when she adjusted the burden wrapped in a shawl on her back that I realized she was carrying a baby, a tiny, pucker-lipped human being whose dull eyes gazed blankly at the fading twilight. I wish I had done something to help that baby and that woman, but I didn't. I just sat there as the store blurred into darkness and tried to ignore the silence they left behind.

"Truly, it's as the priest tells us," Refugio finally said. "No matter how little one has, someone else has less."

"And vice versa," Spoon said.

As if to rekindle our spirits, Refugio lit his Coleman lantern. "Your friend has given me many wonderful gifts," he said.

"It's nothing," Spoon said. "It's Payless. Which reminds me, I brought you a box of ballpoint pens that erase."

"Do they make the little click?"

"As a matter of fact, yes."

"You see?" Refugio said. "He treats —"

At that moment another figure appeared in the doorway.

"Señor Díaz, may a thirsty soldier come in for a sip?"

"Who is that?" Refugio said. "Do I know you?"

"It's Jaimecito Chac, son of Ramón."

"Perhaps another night, Jaimecito. I have friends visiting."

"We marched all the way from San Bartolomeo. I told my fellow soldiers that we would be treated kindly in my town."

"Go to your mother's house," Refugio said.

"Let us in," a man behind Jaimecito said.

"This is not a cantina," Refugio said. "How many of you are there?"

"Just three," Jaimecito said.

"In the interest of good relations between the army and the community, I will serve you one drink," Refugio said.

Spoon greeted the soldiers with a friendly salute, but one of them took an instant aversion to him.

"Is this a man or an overgrown carrot?" the soldier said.

"Corporal Morales, please," Jaimecito said.

"Where does he come from — the planet Mars?" Corporal Morales was short and stocky, and he carried a conspicuous Uzi.

"He comes from the womb of his mother," Refugio said. "Just like you."

Spoon goose-stepped to the counter, belly flopped over it, and popped his head up on the other side. "Let me at him," he said in English. "I'll murder the bum."

"Don't make too big a joke of it," I said.

Refugio served the soldiers at the table, and then he and I quietly toasted the health of Spoon and Magdalena, their children, and their children's children. I've never swallowed hot needles, but that's how the *guaro* tasted, a clear corn liquor with twigs floating in it. I took the smallest sips permissible.

The soldiers didn't even sip. Now and then they'd lift their cups and savor the fragrance of the *guaro* — which smelled like liniment — but they put off drinking, as if the prospect surpassed the experience.

"So what do you think of this election?" Spoon asked Refugio.

"Very kind of you to arrange it," Refugio said.

"Has there been much publicity?"

"Yes, yes. Notices in *La Prensa* and announcements on Radio Atitlán. *Under the auspices of the honorable Dr. Patricio McGuffin.* Very impressive."

"Will many vote?"

Refugio shrugged.

"Will you vote?"

"I hope to."

"How about Hércules?"

Refugio flicked his eyes at the soldiers and lowered his voice. "Our friend is suffering a lot."

"Why?"

"It's not a simple story."

"We've got time."

Refugio checked the soldiers again. They still hadn't drunk. "Our friend has encountered much trouble since you left. The windshield of his truck was broken. His house was cursed. The widow —"

"What do you mean, *cursed?*"

"Someone hung a lizard from the roof of his toolshed. A piece of green thread ran through its mouth and out the tip of its tail. The rumor is that don Pepe hired two shamans from San Blás. Imagine hiring two shamans because you weren't sure which was more powerful."

"Hércules doesn't believe in the curse?" Spoon said.

"No, but the widow does. She asked him to hire his own shaman or move out."

"Incredible," Spoon said.

"Well, it's been bad," Refugio said. "A goat died for no reason. They saw strangers around. The widow drank spoiled mango juice and vomited for a day and a half. But that wasn't the worst part. Her insides bled. I saw the sheets because my wife washed them. She told my wife she lost an unborn child. Please don't mention this. Hércules doesn't know I know."

Refugio grabbed a broom and started sweeping the hard-packed dirt floor. He swept under the feet of the soldiers, who, reluctantly, downed their shots. They didn't budge from the table, however. The corporal held his thumb and forefinger an inch apart. "Just a bit more," he said. "I don't sleep well without it."

"Any other night," Refugio said. "But now we must all go home."

"You leave the store unguarded?" the corporal said.

"My son stays here," Refugio said.

"Then we'll wait for him. We'll keep you company over one more sip."

"That's very kind, but I must close. Tomorrow we'll share a whole liter of *guaro*. Jaimecito, felicitations to your mother and father."

The corporal licked the inside of his cup and complained that he deserved better, but he might have dragged himself away if Hércules hadn't arrived. Hércules seemed to antagonize the corporal just by acknowledging each person in the room with a dignified nod.

"Where have I had dealings with you?" the corporal said, fixing on him as intently as I did.

Hércules looked straight at the corporal as he provided his name, occupation, and place of residence.

"Have you visited San Juan recently?" the corporal asked.

"I was in the vicinity."

"For what reason?"

"My brother-in-law lives there. He asked me to deliver some bread from our cooperative, a few bags of onions."

"Did you drive around a roadblock?"

"I simply took an alternate route."

"Why? Are you working with the ORPA?"

"No."

The corporal whispered to Jaimecito. Jaimecito nodded uneasily. "What is your involvement with the civilian defense patrol?" the corporal said.

"I have none," Hércules said.

"You refuse to serve your community?"

"I serve."

"Then why do you speak against the patrols to your neighbors?"

Spoon vaulted over the counter and swooped down on the

corporal like a bird of prey. "May I tape-record this? I've never recorded an interrogation before."

"The carrot has a tongue," the corporal said. He held out a hand, palm up, not for money, as I first thought, but for documents. Spoon more than obliged. "Here's my passport. And here's a card signed by the President which identifies me as a distinguished guest of the Republic."

The corporal indicated with a brusque wave that he'd seen enough, but Spoon pulled out more papers. "Here's a letter from the local military commissioner, a letter from the regional governor, a copy of my diploma from the University of California. Here's my international driver's license."

"Look at this *yanqui*," the corporal said. "How he behaves. He learns a few words of our language, buys our native clothes, dabbles in our lives as a hobby. *And you stupid Indians encourage him.*"

"Excuse me," Refugio said. "Let's put an end to this bad feeling. Let's drink to each other's health."

"This faggot is going to the lieutenant," the corporal said.

Refugio uncorked the jug. "My friend, believe me, the trouble would fall on your own head. He's a distinguished doctor of science. The lieutenant would not be pleased."

The corporal snarled an obscenity so extreme that Spoon burst out laughing: "The lieutenant can shit in the milk of his mother the whore."

Spoon offered his hand to the corporal. "You and I have much in common. A deep-rooted problem with authority. I'm sorry. I apologize for my uncivilized behavior."

The corporal sneered at Spoon and reached across the table for his Uzi.

Hércules coughed—a dry, cautionary cough. The corporal hesitated.

"Leave us in peace," Hércules said.

"He carries a knife," Jaimecito said to the corporal.

"I carry an Uzi," the corporal said.

"We invited you for a friendly drink," Refugio said. "Please don't abuse our hospitality."

The exertion of wills was almost tangible, like the hum and

spark of wet power lines. Hércules stood poised in the murky lantern light, eyes locked on the corporal's outstretched right hand wavering scant inches from the stock of the Uzi, his own right hand clenched at his side, swinging almost imperceptibly, as if ready, even eager, to strike. I imagined him slinging a hidden knife through the corporal's heart.

"Please accept my apology," Spoon said again.

The corporal ignored him. "Tomorrow afternoon in front of the mayor's office there is a meeting of all able-bodied men between the ages of fourteen and fifty-nine, to discuss the reinvigoration of our civil defense. It would be to your advantage to attend."

The corporal gingerly lifted the Uzi by the strap and led his soldiers out. Jaimecito offered an apologetic curtsy in the doorway.

As soon as they were gone, Spoon checked for Hércules' knife. The long steel blade tapered to a gleaming point. "I lay my balls in a vice to keep you out of trouble and look what you almost do."

Hércules pressed his palms tight together as if in fervent prayer. "These days, my friend, trouble and I are *like this.*"

Traversing the steep mountainside in the moonlight, I crouched low and tried to shield the bulk of my body behind my suitcase. I was certain the embittered corporal would open fire any second. My only doubt was whether I'd hear the shots first, or feel them, or die unable to distinguish. I pictured my gory execution in blood-spattering detail, complete with my mother's collapse at the closed-casket funeral.

Inside Refugio's small house, I sank in front of the fire and kissed my father's cross. Refugio's wife bobbed her head approvingly and went on patting out tortillas. The house consisted of a single windowless smoke-filled room with thatched walls of wattle and daub and a sloped ceiling just tall enough at its highest point to accommodate Spoon, who beamed at Refugio's wife and presented her with a spool of gold ribbon. She gravely turned to Refugio and had him thank Spoon for her. After serving a spicy mush of corn, squash, and hot chili peppers, she lay down with the children on a thin straw mat and pretended not to watch us. Now and then, though, I saw the firelight flicker in her eyes.

Refugio apologized for the meagerness of the meal. "There is a shortage of chickens in the village," he said. "And at the present moment our baby goats are too young to slaughter."

"I have never enjoyed more generous hospitality than here in the home of the Díaz family," Spoon said.

I ate too fast and my mouth caught fire. Three tortillas failed to stop the burning. I looked around for water, but the only thing to drink was *guaro*, so I took a swig, which was like applying iodine to an open wound. My lips threatened to burst into flame. I sucked on my handkerchief. Yet no one seemed to notice my affliction. I had to remind myself that a few minutes earlier I'd been braced for the fatal bullet. How could I let a chili pepper do me in?

"If you need something to wear to the wedding, we can shop in Guatemala City after the election," Spoon was saying. "It would please me to buy you nice suits or whatever."

"Best not to count on us," Hércules said.

"Nonsense," Spoon said.

I was so cold and tired that I didn't care if I offended anyone. I stripped to the waist as quickly as possible; put on two T-shirts, a thermal shirt, a sweater, and a goose-down jacket Spoon had lent me for the trip.

"What do you believe in?" Hércules asked Spoon.

"Beautiful women," Spoon said.

"I'm serious," Hércules said.

"Too much so," Spoon said.

I curled up by the fire and listened to the conversation with my eyes closed. Hércules' raspy voice reminded me of my father. He had the same truck driver's croak.

"I would appreciate your advice, Patricio," he said. "Certain people have asked me to do certain things—things that a man of peace would not normally consider."

"Extreme measures," Refugio said.

"Do you believe that good deeds can produce evil?" Hércules asked. "More important, can evil deeds produce good?"

I tried to imagine Spoon's expression.

"You can't beat good deeds," he said. "Even if they lead to grief. I'm afraid we have to settle for small victories, like this election."

"You know I strive to do the best I can," Hércules said. "Good works will be rewarded, the priest always told me, and I used to believe him. Now I see my life and my country sinking in shit, and the things I do with the best intentions just speed up the process."

"I'm sorry you're having troubles," Spoon said. "Refugio mentioned the curse of the shamans."

"I'm not talking about those old drunks," Hércules said. His voice remained low and gruff. "I'm talking about the troubles I've manufactured myself. The civil defense patrols, for instance. I spoke against them at the last town meeting and now the army is here. No doubt they'll teach some innocent fool a lesson."

Rolling over and sitting up as unobtrusively as possible, I peeked at Hércules' craggy face in the dim light. He wrapped his arms around his chest, as if held captive by his own strength.

"When I arrived in Guatemala, I deeply admired the guerillas," Spoon said. "Their politics, at least in theory, resembled mine. In practice, though, they're almost as bad as the government, and that *almost* is not worth dying for."

Refugio spoke up. "I've always recommended walking away from trouble. These days I recommend running."

"How can a man live with himself when every day he adds to the misery?" Hércules said. "I ask you again — what do you believe in?"

"I suppose I believe in education," Spoon said, stroking his clean-shaven chin. It occurred to me that his passion for late-night conversation had been keeping me awake since we were freshmen in college. "I also believe that the ends never justify the means. You have to take consolation in little things. This election, for instance. Remember how you nagged me to approach Don Hoover? *Help us make elections,* you said. Wasn't that you?"

"Forgive me for criticizing," Hércules said, "but this is not a true election. A true election would be held when all the workers were present."

"What about the notice in *La Prensa*? The announcements on Radio Atitlán?"

"How many seasonal workers read? How many hear the radio? Besides, Patricio, it's still corn-planting season. That's why Refugio will be out in his *milpa* tomorrow. And it's a long trip to La Esperanza. Who can spare the time and expense to go cast a meaningless vote?"

"Suppose there's one chance in a hundred that Hoover wants to improve conditions. Can you afford to waste that chance?"

"If the *patrón* wants to improve conditions, he doesn't need an election."

"Then why has he permitted this one?"

"There are those who say an election is a way to identify your enemies."

Spoon flapped his arms in exasperation. He should have been relieved that Hércules had no interest in the election, but instead he seemed bent on recruiting him. "I won't defend Hoover. He's a businessman. But maybe it's becoming good business to treat the workers better."

"There's no incentive," Hércules said. "As long as the military terrorizes the villages, thousands of *campesinos* will descend on the *fincas*. They will find no saints in charge."

Spoon lurched to his feet. "Sometimes even the illusion of change is better than no change at all."

Hércules poked the glowing embers of the fire with a black stick. "This afternoon I was soaking my bones in the *temescal,* praying for guidance, when Refugio's son ran up and shouted your name. I respect you as a rigorous thinker, Patricio. What I'm saying is that I need a sign. My whole life could pass with nothing."

Spoon paced, stooping, to a smoky corner of the room, where he lit three candles at a shrine to the blessed virgin. Then he paced back with a framed photograph of the current president of Guatemala. Tucked behind the frame, he showed me, were photographs of previous presidents. "The powers that be," he said. "One frame fits all." He turned to Hércules. "Tonight you almost threw your knife, but you didn't. That's what I admire about you—potency mixed with restraint. This country has plenty of cutthroats, but it lacks men who combine judgment and strength."

"Maybe I didn't throw the knife because I couldn't hit anything with it."

"Everybody knows how deadly you are."

"Sometimes a reputation is enough."

Spoon waved the photographs. "It's not my place to tell you what to do. But I will say this. My idea of a hero is someone who bides his time, occupies himself with the small good deeds we were talking about, until the right moment arrives and he acts with greatness."

Hércules broke into a bittersweet smile. "What if the right moment has already arrived, my friend? What if the right moment arrived last week?"

"Armando, help me," Spoon said. "Armando is very wise for an American."

I had no idea what Spoon wanted me to say. The thick smoke that filled the room seemed symptomatic of my confusion. I didn't understand how Spoon could sound so radical in California and so moderate in Guatemala. I wondered what Refugio had meant by *extreme measures.*

"I'm too out of it," I said.

"Explain to Hércules that I'm an anthropologist," Spoon said. "Anthropologists don't meddle. Tell him about Star Trek. The prime directive. Noninterference."

"Are you sure it's interference?" I asked. "Hércules doesn't have to take your advice. Besides, he probably already knows what he wants to do. That's how it works in my family. When my mother wants to do something wild, she asks my sister for advice. When she wants to do something sensible, she asks me."

"And what do I want, please?" Hércules said.

I pointed at Spoon.

"To contribute your honorable presence to the election and to the wedding?" Spoon said.

"If you say so, I'll run," Hércules said. "I'll stand witness for you and your bride. What better way to postpone a difficult decision?"

Refugio patted my wrist. "Your gentle guidance brings to mind the shrewd sayings of my grandmother."

Shortly after Refugio's compliment, I dropped out of the conversation. I couldn't help thinking, as I dry-brushed my teeth and swallowed the toothpaste, that even here in the hinterlands of Guatemala I was still the same Armando, a grandmotherly man of thirty, the saint of the swing shift. My mother used to call me a natural-born peacekeeper when I'd try to cajole her and my father into pretending to get along.

No one had asked what I believed in, but now—conscientiously storing my toothbrush in its plastic case, slipping the case into my dop kit, and stowing the dop kit in my Samsonite next to Sonny Tzoc's package—I realized with disappointment that I harbored no lofty goals, no noble aspirations. I rarely if ever worried about helping others. Settling into the least uncomfortable position the dirt floor permitted, I had to admit that my highest ideal was purely negative: to do as little damage as possible, to inflict the minimum pain.

The smoke at floor level thinned appreciably. The voices of Spoon and Hércules merged with the crackle of the fire. That night I dreamed of riding in a truck with my father.

In real life my father died in a single vehicle collision. It happened, coincidentally or not, less than a month after I'd told him I was dropping out of law school and separating from my wife. The night of his death, before leaving the house, he'd wrapped his pink cross around my trophy on the mantel. Outstanding Boy, Reedley High School. On his way out of town, he'd stopped at Groot's Liquors, where he'd bought a six-pack of Budweiser and a mini-bottle of *Gusano Rojo*. He'd bet old Groot five dollars on the next Giant-Dodger game. Then he'd cruised River Road at better than seventy miles an hour for a long time, long enough to finish four beers and the entire bottle of mescal.

In the dream I sat beside him. He drank in reckless gulps, but he scanned the road carefully. Just before he pressed the accelerator to the floor, he looked over and sighed, as if at last he'd found a safe place to have a fatal accident, and my dream took me elsewhere, as only dreams do.

VII

SKINNY-DIP

*From a height of three or four thousand feet, we
looked down upon a surface shining like a sheet
of molten silver.... There were no associations
connected with this lake; until lately we did not
even know its name; but we both agreed that it
was the most magnificent spectacle we ever saw.*
JOHN LLOYD STEPHENS

Have you ever been lucky enough to recognize your own happiness without ruining it? I enjoyed that rare privilege at Lake
Atitlán, lounging beside Spoon on a rocky beach, curling my
thick fingers into a telescope and looking at the procession of
late afternoon clouds, senatorial in their splendor, inflated with
pomp, yet nimble. The contrast between the vast sky and the intricate contours of my hand seemed miraculous. Only I in the
history of humanity would perceive this particular combination
of clouds and flesh. The stiff wind known as *El Chocomil* lifted off
the lake, the clouds transformed, the pattern of transformation
transformed, and I felt as though I deserved a vacation. I had
nothing with me, no Samsonite, no briefcase. I was unencum-
bered, carefree, refreshed by honest work and healthy steam.

The day had begun unpromisingly. I'd woken up huddled
on a cold dirt floor surrounded by smoke. Outside, though, the
rising sun had glinted off the chicken-wire pen where Refugio's
daughters were crawling after a trio of baby goats while Refugio's wife weaved a green *mantilla* on her back-strap loom.
Spoon had been in a hurry to join Refugio in his *milpa*, but I'd
lingered for a breath of sweet air. A hummingbird throbbed
above a red hibiscus. The night before, when I'd climbed the
hill with such grisly expectations, death had seemed close
enough to touch. This brilliant morning, skidding and sliding
down the eroded hillside after Spoon, dodging tree stumps
and rodent holes, I felt supremely grateful to have survived.

Refugio had just finished burning off last year's stubble when Spoon and I had hiked up to his rugged field. Smoke was still rising from the ground. A flock of grackles swarmed after the sluggish worms unearthed by the fire. We'd worked as a team: Refugio would dig a hole the depth of his thumb, I would drop in four different kinds of seeds, and Spoon would refill the hole with dirt. Soon, despite the steep slope and the constant bending, we'd developed a comfortable rhythm. Refugio had entertained us with his observations. He'd said that a *milpa* was only good for three years, each year worse than the previous one. He'd dug up an ant the length of a Bic pen. "These *zompopos* eat everything," he'd said. "But they like pesticide best." Hércules had brought us a pitcher of cold coffee spiked with lemon juice, and after he'd joined us, the work had zipped by. It had been a distinct pleasure to push the last seeds down into the last hole.

To reward our diligence, Refugio had fired up his *temescal,* the native Guatemalan steam bath. He'd shown us how to arrange the stones to regulate the temperature of the fire. He'd explained with patience and delight which wood burned coolest, which herbs best cured gout, arthritis, a broken heart. He'd said that the *temescal* was called *abuelita,* little grandmother, because it kept its children warm.

"I didn't know that," Hércules said. "Are you sure you don't make these things up?"

We'd soaked in the steam with our clothes on, even though the heat was fierce. Refugio had poured water mixed with sage and fennel on the hot stones.

"How do you like this Guatemala of mine?" Spoon had asked me in a whisper.

The four of us had sweated together in silence, lost in our separate thoughts.

Afterwards, Refugio had gone to the meeting of the civilian defense patrol. Hércules had decided to avoid trouble and wash his truck instead. Spoon and I had hiked about a mile and a half across a gully, over a hill, and down through a stand of skinny oaks to the shore of the most beautiful lake I've ever seen — and that includes National Geographic specials on TV. Spoon had draped his wet clothes over a low branch, and self-consciously I had done the same. Even though we were the only ones around, it seemed daring to lie on the beach in my boxer shorts next to Spoon in his tiger-striped bikini briefs. I appreciated our seclusion, our shared solitude, our pleasure in each other's company. Watching a cloud turn into a goose, a flock of geese, I basked in our friendship—until I heard Spoon moan into his tape recorder.

"I'm going through a bit of a crisis here," he confided to the built-in microphone. "What we anthropologists call a rite of passage, a liminal period, betwixt and between. Which means I don't know my ass from my elbow."

I swung my hand-telescope in his direction. He lay in yogi-like contortion, bony ankle crossed on bony knee, freckled foot dangling toward the waterline. The tape recorder captured the splash of choppy waves, the swish of oak trees in the wind.

"It's the old beware-of-what-you-want-you-may-get-it syndrome," he said. "I'm about to become a husband, a professor, a published author. Imagine. I'm going to occupy a position. I won't float anymore."

Sometimes when you're with a person you've known for a long time, that person will say exactly what you've been thinking, and your connection perceptibly strengthens. This was the opposite of that experience. I looked out at the boundless lake extending farther than the horizon, and I had a sense of the limitations of my perspective.

"What's your worst fear?" Spoon said. He stared at me while I considered the question. "Be honest. Please."

"I guess I'm afraid of losing control," I said.

"Are you kidding?" he said.

"No. Seriously. Sometimes it's like there's this bum locked inside me, this utterly slack soul, and if I slip—"

"You want to hear my biggest fear?" Spoon said. "My biggest fear is getting fat. Becoming a fat-assed yuppie slut like my brother." He jumped up and began to pace. His shadow was longer than he was. "Did you notice this pile of rocks?" He pointed to a mound of smooth stones under the oak where our clothes were hanging. "The late baker of Santa Catalina. Nice guy. Our age. Drowned in the seaweed right out there." He snapped his fingers furiously. The wind was dying down, the sun was setting, but he flailed away at full speed. "In the mood for a sad story?" he said.

"If you'll stay put," I said.

The clouds turned from white to pink to purple, the surface of the lake grew calm, and Spoon paced the beach in his tiger-striped briefs. "When I was eight years old," he said, tape recorder bouncing against his bare chest, "we lived on the island of Crete. I don't know how my father wangled that assignment. There was nothing strategic about the place. I think it had to do with the Bay of Pigs. Most of the folks involved in that fiasco got tucked away in the boondocks. At any rate, my mother always wanted to live in Greece. It was the first and only assignment she was happy with.

"Unfortunately, my grandmother fractured her hip or some damn thing, and my mother had to fly to Virginia to take care of her. To make matters worse, our housekeeper Georgina had already gone on vacation. So my father was running the ship, and he'd promised us a major expedition, but late that night the office called. Terrible emergency. Urgent that he come in. I don't know if they told him over the phone, but President Kennedy had been shot."

Spoon slackened his pace. "My brother was ten, I was eight, Mary Alice five. My father could have brought us in with him, but he didn't. He just issued his usual orders, except this time he issued them to me instead of to my mother or my brother. He was pissed off at my brother for some reason. I can't remember why. Anyway, he said, 'I leave you in complete command. Make no decisions.' We both saluted."

Outlined against the darkening sky, Spoon demonstrated the salute. "Well, the next morning we made our own breakfast and played inside for awhile, and then we decided it would probably be okay if we went on our expedition. There was this old abandoned house on a hill overlooking the sea, and we played there for awhile, and then my brother and I decided to walk the wall that ran down to the water.

"This wall served no purpose whatsoever. It was just there, six feet high and maybe a hundred yards long. Whitewashed. We rolled a big rock up to it and climbed up. We told Mary Alice to wait by the rock."

Spoon stopped. He sank down with his back to the lake and wrapped his arms around his knees. He seesawed back and forth, almost as if in a trance.

"It was weird," he said. "When I saw her lying there by the rock, I knew she was hurt, but I pretended she was faking. I jumped down right next to her and started tickling her ribs. I said: 'Get up, you little faker. Get up. Get up.' Spoon tucked his head between his knees and stared down at the dirt. When he finally spoke again, his voice was oddly sweet. "She was still breathing and everything. But she went into a coma that lasted weeks and weeks. I remember the phrase the doctor used. Suspended animation. And I was confused because animation meant cartoons.

"That day, though, I held her little grubby hand while my brother ran back to the house. Just to finish off the farce, there was this sergeant there. My father had sent this sergeant out to baby-sit, only he'd paid a visit to his girlfriend first. Something like that. He lost his stripes over the deal. And my father, when he met us at the hospital, blamed the sergeant more than me. He said it was a chain of circumstances, from my grandmother's hip to the assassination of the President. We talked for a long time at the hospital. Someday, he said, I'd be a big, big hero. As if that would make up for it."

Spoon looked up and cracked his neck. The sky was dark blue now. The purple clouds held the last lingering light of day.

"I'm afraid I'll never be a hero. I'm afraid I'll just be a husband the rest of my life."

"Marriage can be heroic," I said.

"I want to ring the bell, plug the dike, cut the knot, pull the sword from the stone, die on the cross—is that asking too much?"

He lay back down and I lay down and we watched the stars come out. It was getting cold, but the ground was warmer than the air. After awhile, without trying to, I reached a decision.

"I think tomorrow I might take that package to Sonny Tzoc's brother. Would that be okay with you?"

"If you want," Spoon said. "An adventure wouldn't do you any harm. In fact, let's go for a swim."

"That's okay," I said.

Spoon peeled off his bikini briefs.

"The baker drowned," I said.

"I can't believe you're afraid of losing control," Spoon said. "You never lose control. You never do anything wild."

He ran splashing into the lake. I heard him whoop, slap the water, and call my name. Eventually, I hung up my boxers and waded in after him.

The dark water shocked, soothed, and supported all at once. It made having a body worthwhile.

I swam out to Spoon and we swam out farther, toward a portion of the lake filled with phosphorescence. He did an easy sidestroke for my sake. I'm not much at home in the water—drowning was one of those fears my mother managed to communicate through osmosis—but I loved this newfound buoyancy, this weightlessness. The phosphorescence looked like neon strings in the distance.

"Maybe it's the spirit of the lake," Spoon said. "According to legend, the spirit of the lake seeks out tired souls. It lures them down to the bottom and keeps them as servants."

"Was the baker out this far?" I said.

"The locals don't really swim in the lake," Spoon said. "They just bathe. The earlier in the day, the better. They say the impurities build up as the day wears on. Not to mention all the villages dump their sewage at sunset."

"Thanks for telling me," I said.

"Hey, what time is it?" Spoon said, which seemed like an odd question until I noticed my Timex. A cloud had formed under the crystal. In a burst of spontaneity, I dropped the watch into the lake.

"How's that for wild?" I said.

"Not bad," he said. "I'm glad you're here."

The phosphorescence disappeared after the moon rose over

the mountains, but I didn't mind. The entire lake glistened. The moonlit trees reminded me of Christmas. We swam back slowly, searching out the warmest currents. I'd never gone skinny-dipping before. I'd have to say I recommend it.

VIII

CHOCOLATE AND MULE

caminante, no hay camino
se hace camino al andar
ANTONIO MACHADO

The first twenty-four hours of the longest day of my life began in the middle of the night when I woke up refreshed, with none of the usual sluggishness. By the flickering light of *ocotes* (thin strips of pine that burn like torches), I helped grind corn for the breakfast tortillas. Refugio said a prayer before we ate:

> *We who are made of maize—*
> *yellow maize and white maize—*
> *thank you for the gift of maize*
> *the gift of life*
> *the gift of water and sky.*

Crowded into the cab of Hércules' Peterbilt, we drove in darkness all the way to Sololá. I was so euphoric I shouted into Refugio's ear that what I wanted most in life was to visit new places, to plunge into the unknown and see what happened.

"Plunge with God," Spoon said when they dropped me off at the bus stop next to the marketplace. "You intrepid traveler, you."

In the damp gray dawn, a ragged boy bent to shine my Hush Puppies. A toothless newspaper vendor assured me that the bus to Chichicastenango would arrive shortly. An hour later he re-assured me: *hay viene al ratito.* I didn't mind waiting. Once the mist burned off, the marketplace lit up like a dazzling mosaic: mats laid out with cabbages, onions, fabrics, yarns, bundles of roots, mounds of red powder, candles, and spectacularly dressed Guatemalan women. I caught a glimpse across the way of Spoon and Hércules talking to a man in greasy overalls, and then my bus rolled up, belching black smoke.

My seatmate put his head between his legs and spit twice a minute until he fell asleep. I wedged my suitcase across my lap and tried to keep my Hush Puppies clear of the shifting puddle of spit. Eventually, I stopped trying. I just let my mind wander, seduced by the pleasures of reverie.

Bus travel in Guatemala teaches resignation. You're at the mercy of forces far beyond your control, so why fight it? In Chichicastenango I waited two hours for the bus to Santa Cruz del Quiché, where I waited nearly three hours for a bus to the vicinity of Maluatla. Basically, the longer the wait, the shorter the ride. The shorter the ride, the more stops you make. The more stops you make, the faster you go between stops. On the last leg, I mistakenly stood up front and witnessed at point-blank range the driver's preference for neutral on steep downhill stretches and his pathological distrust of brakes. The worst part was dodging a donkey cart just before we hurtled across the narrow bridge into Chebaj. I actually considered praying. As soon as the bus coasted to a stop, I staggered off.

There was no bus service to Maluatla, the proprietor of an open-air food stand informed me, but the walk was not far. A teenage boy estimated three kilometers; a wrinkled nun, eleven.

"It's exactly four kilometers, sir," the proprietor said. He had a toothbrush mustache and very sharp teeth.

"Is there a path?" I asked.

"Oh, yes, there's quite a path," he said. "You know the bridge?"

"I'll never forget it."

"Just turn left at the bridge and keep on straight. Perfectly straight. You can't miss Maluatla." When the proprietor smiled, his teeth pointed in conflicting directions and his pink gums glistened. He had no reason to fool me, but I felt as though we were speaking in code and I was missing the real message.

"How long does it take to get there?" I said.

"It depends on how you walk, of course. Maybe an hour, maybe more."

It was about four o'clock in the afternoon. I'd left Refugio's well before dawn, but I'd traveled less than two hundred miles and I still had considerable distance to go.

The proprietor charged the boy and the nun a quetzal each for their sodas, but when I gave him a five-quetzal note, he just stuffed it in his apron and sat down on a crate.

"Where's my change?" I said.

Grudgingly, he uncrumpled four worn one-quetzal notes and spread them out in front of me. I picked up three of them and then put one back.

The overgrown path just short of the bridge rose sharply through dense willow trees and vines. I looked around for someone to confirm my directions. The stillness of the empty bridge seemed almost supernatural. I took a tentative step down the path, reminded myself I was intrepid, and plunged, whistling, because in Yosemite Betsy and I always whistled to let the bears know we were coming—never surprise bears or the local equivalent.

We used to fish on those trips. We'd find a pool where the stream slowed down and fly-cast for trout, and after a while we'd start to notice what had been there the whole time: a rock shaped like a pumpkin, a nest in the crotch of a spruce. That's how the hike went at first. I gradually tuned in to the pulsing buzz of cicadas and the cry of hidden birds. I saw grasshoppers, butterflies, mottled frogs. It was a rugged climb, but my Samsonite felt light and the path was easy to follow—until I reached the fork.

All of a sudden I heard a rustle in the underbrush. A snake slithered up the gnarled trunk of a tree. My awareness intensified, as if the volume had been turned up not only on the cicadas and frogs, but also on the nervous voices clamoring in my head. Had I blown it? Had the proprietor tricked me?

I forced myself to study both forks, each about as wide as a jeep. The left fork went off toward where I figured Maluatla should be, but the right fork seemed more traveled. I thought of Claude's parting shot: "Those boys got no idea what they're getting into."

Stalling for somebody to come along, I drank a little water from my plastic canteen. My sweat came along—palms, armpits, back of the neck. A mosquito came along and bit me on the cheek as I squashed it. The corporal with the Uzi came along, lined me up in his sights, and pulled the trigger—or was that my imagination? Half paralyzed by self-consciousness, I wiped my face with a handkerchief, dabbed on a few drops of insect repellent, and moved the canister of mace from my Samsonite to my breast pocket before proceeding with due caution up the left fork.

So much for the pleasures of reverie. As my suitcase grew heavier and the mosquitoes multiplied, I asked myself what was the worst that could happen. That strategy had served me well in law school, but now the worst possibilities seemed far more gruesome. I envisioned a poisonous snake biting through my jeans, a suspicious farmer hacking me to death with a machete, a trigger-happy soldier dropping his automatic weapon in embarrassment after a dozen bullets had riddled my body. Yes, I could die on this errand, or, any second now, I could arrive at the home of Sebastiano Tzoc with a package from his kindly brother who lived in a pink stucco duplex in Glen Park. I'd be embraced by the family, fed chocolate and coffee, *appreciated*, a good man doing a good deed.

By the time I reached the second fork, the patches of sky visible through the canopy of branches had turned a pale, pale blue. *Todo recto*, the proprietor had said. Straight all the way.

Flipping a coin to decide which fork to take, I somehow tripped over my suitcase. It occurred to me on my knees that if Spoon had been along I would have felt much calmer, not because of any special confidence in him but just because whatever happened to us would happen to *us*. Now my own private fate had a chance to catch me alone, and that prospect was frightening.

I made a deal with myself to take five hundred more steps. I counted out loud to prevent doubts from forming.

On step fifty-four, I heard the thud of a sizable animal. My first instinct was to whistle, but my lips were too dry. My second instinct was to dive into the underbrush, but instead I stood absolutely still, remembering my mother's advice about bees: if you don't move, they won't sting you. I didn't move.

Oddly enough, the boy and mule who appeared in the somber light of dusk followed bee logic and trudged past me without a quiver of interest.

"Wait!" I finally shouted. (The Spanish word for *wait* also means *hope*.) "I'm lost. Can you help me?"

Straw hat pulled low over his forehead, the boy chewed a stringy root without changing his implacable expression.

"I'm looking for Maluatla," I said.

He spoke a few words in an Indian language.

"Maluatla?" I said again. I pointed in the direction I'd been heading.

He thrust his chin the opposite way. When I just stood there, he tugged my shirtsleeve and clicked his tongue to get the mule started.

At the crossroads he aimed me up the other fork and said a word I didn't understand at first; his pronunciation of Maluatla sounded like a hiccup that more or less rhymed with *bottle*.

"How far?" I asked. I held my hands close together and then wide apart.

He held his hands close together.

"Thank you," I said. I didn't have balloons or ballpoint pens, so I gave him ten quetzals. "I hope this doesn't offend you." I wanted to talk, whether he understood me or not.

He definitely understood my need for company. He folded the bill into a tiny rectangle, hid it in his sock, and turned the mule around.

We reached a blacktopped road within ten minutes. Several men armed with sticks, hoes, and machetes stood guard at the outskirts of Maluatla. They didn't scare me, maybe because I was too flabbergasted by the sight of a paved road.

"Does this road go to Chebaj?" I asked.

"Straight all the way. But one shouldn't travel at night."

"No," I said. "I'm coming from Chebaj."

"On the old trail? The new road is really much better, sir."

"I'm sure that's true."

The spokesman of the group translated for the others. His gestures made clear what he must be saying: this stranger preferred the old trail — imagine.

"I'm an American," I said. "A friend of the brother of Sebastiano Tzoc. Can you please tell me where he lives?"

The spokesman looked down at the ground for several

seconds. He repeated the name of Sebastiano Tzoc to the others and they all stared at the ground. "We'll take you to don Lázaro," the spokesman announced, as if the decision had been reached telepathically.

Maluatla was a much larger town than I expected. It had four street lamps, a Red Cross dispensary, and a large public square complete with benches, shade trees, and a gazebo. Three women knelt at the altar of an open-air church, but otherwise the streets were deserted, except for the civilian defense patrol, the boy and the mule, and me.

We stopped at the only house with a wall around it. One of the men rattled the handle of his hoe against the bars of the wrought-iron gate. An ancient Indian woman asked our business. They sent her back for don Lázaro, who, after a long delay, strolled out with a tall glass of beer. He was grotesquely fat. His gold rings and gold watch glinted in the yellow light from the corner street lamp. I noticed with shock that his Rolex watch was identical to Sonny's. "How may I serve you?" he said.

"Can you help me find Sebastiano Tzoc?"

"What is your business with him?"

The Rolex made me cautious. "I am an acquaintance of Sebastiano's brother in the United States. I bring . . . greetings."

"You have traveled a great distance to be thwarted in your purpose, but unfortunately Mr. Tzoc disappeared several months ago. I say *unfortunately*, although, to be perfectly frank, it was not a great loss for me personally. Mr. Tzoc had begun to plot against the government."

Faint lights seemed to hover on the periphery of my field of vision. I grabbed the bars of the gate for support. "What about the rest of his family? Where are they?"

"As a matter of fact, his family moved down to the capital. Or up to Mexico. One son remained, but he also was subversive — or crazy. He was last seen right over there, howling like a dog atop the church. Such a dog runs away or gets put out of its misery."

My head tingled. "Excuse me, but where's the nearest hotel?"

"Mrs. Burgos usually accommodates passers-through, but she's away visiting her cousin."

"Can I buy food anywhere around here?"

"No, but I'll give you some. Concha! Pack some tortillas for the stranger."

"Please, let me pay."

"Unthinkable," he said, but I pulled out the wad of bills Spoon had given me and three loose fifties fluttered to the ground. Scrambling to pick them up, I had an uncanny impression of don Lázaro smacking his lips, even though I had my back to him.

"If you wish to stay here, you're welcome," he said. "I would offer the same accommodations to any needy traveler."

"Thanks for your generosity," I said.

The maid brought out a bundle of tortillas small enough to fit through the bars of the gate.

"The porch at Mrs. Burgos's house should be dry tonight," don Lázaro said, "but look out for scorpions in the corners."

As I tottered to a bench in the plaza, an owl hooted in the distance. I'd never heard an owl sound quite so mournful before.

"The house of Mrs. Burgos doesn't interest you?" the spokesman of the civilian defense patrol said.

"May I stay here?"

"It's a violation of curfew."

"I won't sleep, I promise."

The entire civilian defense patrol discussed the matter. The money in my pocket probably would have supported them for months, but I trusted them more than I trusted don Lázaro.

They recommended the empty school up the hill, behind the church. The boy carried my suitcase. The mule followed him. I said good night to the civilian defense patrol and followed the mule.

I was tired, hungry, and oddly elated. At least I'd have a story to tell Spoon. After I shined my flashlight over every inch of the schoolhouse without finding a scorpion, the boy and I shared don Lázaro's stale tortillas. The boy contributed a dozen green chili peppers the size and shape of golf tees. They weren't as molten as Refugio's chilies, but they burned my whole stomach, providing a gratifying illusion of fullness. Propped against my suitcase in the corner farthest from the door, I was ready to sit up all night. Tomorrow would come and I would survive. "Thanks to don Lázaro for our delicious main course," I said, and shined the flashlight on the piece of waxed paper the tortillas had been wrapped in. "Thanks to you, my laconic friend, for the piquant vegetable dish." I shined the flashlight on the boy, who barely blinked. "Thanks to the Hush Puppy Company for their excellent footwear. Thanks to my mother for this incomparable mace." I doused the flashlight and went on blabbering in the dark. It was the first time in years I'd felt the spirit of prayer. "You don't have a piece of chocolate, by any chance? I smell chocolate. Chocolate and mule . . ."

I woke up alert, every nerve straining, every muscle taut. My head and neck were twisted awkwardly against my suitcase, but I didn't move. I was sure that an intruder stood over me with a gun, and equally sure that my mind was just playing tricks. I opened my eyes and saw in the darkness an even darker shape, a black combat boot, its brass eyelets catching the only light in the room.

I X

DESIRE UNDER THE BOLA TREE

Love stinks.

J. GEILS

Meanwhile, back at the ranch house, I, unfaithful Anglo companion Patrick, was conscientiously proofreading my dissertation by the light of a kerosene lantern.

Okay, I'm a sucker for a classic transition. I wasn't really at the ranch house, I was at one of the nearby shacks. And it wasn't really meanwhile, it was several hours earlier in the evening. To be honest, I wasn't really proofreading, I was more just contemplating the lameness of my words.

But the lantern was real. And the tiresome bugs circling around it. At least they weren't mosquitoes. They were like moths, only smaller. Quiet bugs. Easy to squash. And I remember thinking that there was nothing in my dissertation as real as these bugs. There was nothing of the desolation I felt, the desolation anyone would feel, watching bug shadows flicker across the corrugated walls of this shack.

If Armando had been with me, I'm sure he would have provided some account of what happened on this particular night at La Esperanza. But Armando was *tied up,* so to speak. And so, in the interest of truth, justice, and bad taste, I'm filling in this gap in his story.

I was watching bug shadows and contemplating lameness when I heard the siren song of a motor vehicle maneuvering down the steep road to the hacienda. Praise the Lord. Refugio and Hércules had gone off to campaign among the resident workers, and after a few hours solo I was longing to be rescued. You know how sometimes when you're alone you start to hyper-think? Just ducking outside—practically crawling to fit through the low doorway—I thought about how often the average Indian stooped, the possible connection between stooping and low self-esteem, the woeful absence of this insight from my dissertation. Luckily, the sky was filled with distracting stars and I had company. Magdalena's Buick pulled in front of the hacienda, and out stepped my beloved. Not to mention her wonderdog, Aunt Martha. They didn't see me gliding down the footpath in the moonlight. I watched Magdalena look up at the sky and stretch. Her body assumed the most tantalizing position. And I realized as I broke into a trot that even though I had been longing for someone to rescue me, I hadn't been longing for Magdalena in particular, and that distinction put a funny spin on my pleasure. Aunt Martha barked. I tossed off a sophisticated rejoinder:

"Hey, stranger. New in town?"

Magdalena offered her hands and held me at a distance. "I've missed you," she said. She seemed to mean it.

"I'm glad," I said. "But you shouldn't be out driving at night."

"I need your measurements for the tuxedo," she said.

"Magdalena, baby, sweetheart, you didn't risk your life for that?"

"I had a flat tire," she said. "You know what are the lug nuts?"

"Yes, I know what are the lug nuts."

"They were very tight. I had to try for a long time to pry them loose."

"Magdalena, seriously, you could get killed out there."

She touched my lips with her finger, which I kissed and licked and sucked. Aunt Martha panted beside us. Only Magdalena didn't pant.

"I need to measure you," she said, strictly matter of fact.

"Yes, please, come measure me," I said. I swiveled my hips à la Elvis, but I swear she missed the implication. She was very literal-minded, I decided as we strolled arm in arm back to the shack. When she asked why I didn't stay at the hacienda, I said that the foreman had bad breath, and she squinched her eyebrows, perplexed. It wasn't a problem of language or culture—it was just a problem. And yet despite her solemnity, she seemed utterly desirable.

She measured my sleeve length with yellow measuring tape.

Inhaling the fragrance of her hair, I could hardly wait for the inseam. To my eternal sorrow, Refugio poked his head inside the doorway at the least opportune moment. Aunt Martha started barking.

"Come in. Come in," I said.

Magdalena quieted Aunt Martha to a fierce growl.

"We don't wish to disturb you," Refugio said as he stepped backwards into Hércules, who begged our pardon.

"I insist," I said. "May I present my *novia?*"

"It's a pleasure," Magdalena said, awkwardly restraining Aunt Martha by the collar.

Refugio doffed his hat and bowed. Hércules clasped his hands together and nodded like a modest young priest.

Aunt Martha refused to sit. The damn dog was prejudiced against Indians, which made it difficult for Magdalena to finish measuring me. She had to straddle Aunt Martha between her knees while I tried to cover the awkwardness with talk. No one else would say anything. Magdalena quickly stretched the tape around my waist and down my leg. It didn't approach the erotic experience I'd had in mind, but it was enough to embarrass Refugio, if not Hércules. I invited them again to come to our wedding. Magdalena finally chimed in, polite, even gracious, but a little too formulaic for my taste. She didn't show any real feeling until she asked about Armando. "You let him travel alone?" she said. I estimated his measurements—rather unflatteringly, it turned out. Once she wrote them in the notebook, she was ready to leave.

"Walk me to my car," she said.

"You just got here," I said.

She looked at me. Somehow, with the barest inflection of eyebrows and lips, she imparted an eloquent message. *We don't want to argue. Not in front of your friends. We don't want to argue at all.*

I restrained myself until we were outside. This was the first time we'd rubbed each other the wrong way. We'd been living in a vacuum. Reality—the friction of the real world—suddenly seemed to switch on out there, looming, dangerous, immense as the night. The stars winked above us like the adult version of connect-the-dots. In spite of my frustration, I felt supercharged. Here, now, for better or worse, we were alive together.

"Stay with me," I said. "I want to hold you. Let's lie under the stars and talk until the sun comes up. I need to be close to you."

"Oh, Patricio, I wish I could make you happy."

"You can," I said. I kissed the top of her head, her eyebrows, the bridge of her nose.

She raised her watch between us. "I should be halfway home by now."

"But you're here," I said. I rested my hand on the small of her back, but didn't press her against me. I knew I had to go slow. I guided her toward the deeper, more secluded darkness under the branches of the bola tree. Aunt Martha sniffed at our ankles.

"I'm sorry," Magdalena said. "It's the tire's fault. The flat tire devoured our time."

I was sure I heard regret in her voice. I heard desire. "Just stay," I said.

"My behavior is scandalous enough already. Besides, I have a thousand things to do tomorrow. I only drove out here because I wanted to see you."

"Why did you want to see me?" I asked. I was fishing for a compliment, I admit it, but she only looked away from me and shrugged. "Not to touch me?" I whispered. "Not to put your hands all over my body under the guise of taking measurements?"

"Perhaps to take measurements is why I came. I don't know. I can't say. I'm worried, Patricio." She lay her head against my chest, but it wasn't the contact I wanted.

I kissed her on the neck, the smooth underside of her chin. I kissed her eyelids, the tender spot under her eyes, the dimpled corners of her mouth. I kissed her lips, but they wouldn't soften. They wouldn't give. And then I did something pathetic. I got down on my knees and wrapped my arms around her waist. "Do you love me?" I said. I had never asked that question of anyone. So I must have been desperate. And yet I still expected her to throw herself at me in a fit of passion.

She ran her fingers through my hair and hummed a tuneless consolation song. I buried my face in her denim skirt. She trembled, but didn't pull away.

"Do you love me?" I said again. I couldn't help myself.

"Of course," she said.

"Sometimes I'm afraid I don't know you," I said.

"Of course you don't know me. We have years for that."

"Then what's wrong?" I untucked her blouse and kissed her belly button. I pulled her down beside me and she cooperated, more or less. She gave me her body but not her spirit. I don't mean we had sex—heaven forbid!—I mean she let me press myself against her for a few awkward seconds until Aunt Martha poked her nose in and started licking us.

"She thinks we're playing," Magdalena said.

"She's wrong," I said. "But it's nice to be given the benefit of the doubt."

Magdalena placed my hand over her heart and held it there. I felt the strength of her heartbeat, the warmth of her flesh.

"I'd better go," she said.

"You might as well," I said.

And that's the way it was back at the ranch house.

X

YOU DESERVE A BREAK TODAY

Slander is worse than death.
GUATEMALAN PROVERB

Lying there in the dark with my eyes slit open, I struggled to quiet my heart. It drowned out every other sound, even the tumultuous rush of blood pounding at my temples. *If you don't move, they won't sting you,* I thought. I realized that whatever happened I would remain completely passive. I was incapable of action.

The boot nudged me in the solar plexus. A woman spoke in a low voice. "Come. Please."

"Why?" I said, not with defiance, but with the naive curiosity of a child.

"It's not safe here," she said.

"For whom?" I said.

"Shut up," a man said. He stomped across the schoolroom and jerked me to my feet.

"There's no reason to hurt him," the woman said.

"He's pure shit," the man said.

He yanked my arms behind me and tied them with wire. A wide strip of tape was used to cover my eyes. The man and woman argued about who should carry my suitcase. He smelled like gunpowder and she smelled like cloves. The tape crackled again; the suitcase handle was placed in my right hand and tightly wrapped. I heard the woman whisper in an Indian language, lots of *sh* and *ch* sounds. As I was shoved through the doorway past the mule, I imagined the woman comforting the boy, telling him he was dreaming now and in the morning he would forget the dream. Then I tripped over something and landed hard on my left shoulder.

The blindfold was my only consolation as I stumbled along, hunched forward to improve my balance in the pitch dark. The major artery in my throat constricted so violently I felt the blood shoot upward with every heartbeat. I struggled to bring my body under control. The ground receded and swelled. The suitcase banged against my heels. I slipped on a loose rock, tumbled over, tried to break the fall with my knees, and smashed my nose. The darkness turned yellow and woozy. I was picked up and propelled onward.

"Quiet," the woman said. I didn't understand what she meant until I heard myself snuffling. My nose was clogged. Clogged with blood. I concentrated on my balance, breathed as discreetly as possible, swallowed what blood I could. Even an act as simple as swallowing became difficult.

The third time I fell, the man tore off my blindfold. The one assurance that they intended to keep me alive was suddenly gone, along with patches of my eyebrows. The night was still dark. No starlight or moonlight penetrated the trees. After awhile, though, I started to *hear* better without the blindfold. The sound of the footsteps in front of me offered clues to the terrain. Once I figured out what to listen for—tramp of dirt, crunch of stone, sudden alterations of pace or stride—I stopped losing my balance. I had a long opportunity to wonder if I would live to see the sun come up.

I also wondered if this could be an elaborate joke, the prelude to a wild surprise party. Every possibility attracted its opposite. My self-consciousness was extreme, as if sheer volume of thought might put a safe distance between me and my plight. Gradually, I distinguished the darkness of the sky from the darkness of the trees. When we reached a clearing at the base of a hill, I could just make out a pair of goalposts as we walked under them. Drifting between the pale uprights was a cloud of black smoke.

No one showed much interest in our arrival. One man went on shaving, another repaired a boot. A teenage girl in camouflage fatigues patted out tortillas. Somehow the camp reminded me of the welfare office in the Mission: everyone awake looked bored—except for my escorts (I preferred not to think of them as *captors*), who paraded me up to the fire as if they deserved applause.

What they got was indifference. The shaving man stared into the fire as if it were a mirror and scraped at his stubbly beard without benefit of soap or even water. He was short and wiry, with close-cropped white hair and a sad mouth. He seemed utterly unaware of our presence—of anyone's presence—until the bolder of my escorts worked up the nerve to address him.

"Commandante," she said. "This stranger visited the house of the fat one. He claims to be a *compañero* of the brother of Sebastiano Tzoc."

The commandante distractedly waved his straight razor in my direction. "Your papers," he said.

I jutted my chin at my front left pocket, the safest place to carry a wallet, according to Dear Abby.

"Clara," the commandante said.

Clara of the soothing whisper and the scent of cloves reached into my pocket from behind. She had to lean over my suitcase. Her chin brushed lightly against my back. In that uncomfortably intimate position, it occurred to me that Dear Abby's wisdom no longer applied. Nothing was safe. Just seeing the jagged scar on Clara's wrist put me in danger. I didn't want to know her name or her identifying features. I didn't want anyone to have a reason to kill me.

Watching the commandante paw through my wallet—driver's license, employee building pass, emergency twenty-dollar bill—I wished that I carried family pictures, any personal scrap that might win sympathy. My passport was equally unwinning, blank except for the green Guatemalan entrance stamp. Years ago, my wife had filled out my passport application in hopes of enticing me to New Zealand. We'd squandered fifty precious dollars on that passport. This passport. I should have gone to New Zealand when I had the chance, I thought. My odds of survival would have been better.

"*Estudiante?*" the commandante said, squinting at a word in the passport.

I blinked back tears, tears of blessed relief. I was sure that any person who could derive *estudiante* from *student* would spare my life. I confused intelligence with mercy.

"I'm not a student anymore. I'm a—" Panic shut me up.

What if my job sounded bad here? What if they viewed me as a cog in the infernal capitalist machine? "I'm a teacher," I said. "I teach English and Spanish to little children in California."

"Ah, California," the commandante said.

My other escort, the goon of goons, glared at me, full of contempt. "Liar," he said. "I hate teachers. They lie worse than priests."

"Calm yourself, Ernesto," the commandante said.

Ernesto performed a scornful bow. He broke down his Kalachnikov while the commandante asked me questions. When I explained that I was delivering a package to a friend, the commandante had Clara untie my arms and fetch the suitcase. She popped the latches for him. Perched on a small block of wood, he unpacked my belongings one item at a time, scrutinizing even the elastic band of my boxer shorts in the unsteady light of the fire.

No gun was aimed my way, and the sky had lightened just enough to reveal a cluster of aguacatillo trees on the hill behind the camp. Everyone probably knew a dozen escape routes up that hill, through those trees—everyone except me.

The commandante saved Sonny's package for last. Ernesto refused to unwrap it, so the task fell to Clara, who treated the twine and brown paper as precious commodities, untying every pesky knot and patiently fingernailing every piece of tape, just as my mother would have. I was curious to see what I was risking my life for. What does a family in the United States send to a family in Guatemala?

The first thing the commandante pulled out was a plastic coffee cup imprinted with the slogan "You Deserve a Break Today." He twisted off the no-spill lid, sniffed inside the cup, popped the lid back on.

Next came a carton of Marlboros and a carton of Kools, my mother's brand. Several men who had been sleeping some distance from the fire zeroed in on the cigarettes. One whistled; another clapped; a third recoiled as if ashamed of his own covetousness. The word *menthol* was pronounced in Spanish, surrounded by Indian words. I inched backwards, almost tempted to try to slip away until I noticed Ernesto pretending not to keep track of me while he wiped the barrel of his Kalachnikov with a greasy rag.

The cigarettes were followed by four Giants baseball caps, a Golden Gate Bridge ashtray, half a dozen Alcatraz T-shirts, a Frisbee, a cassette tape of Michael Jackson's *Thriller,* and a bag of chocolate kisses. I licked my lips. I had been starving for those kisses without knowing it. My heartbeat had steadied, the numbness was leaving my arms, and it seemed almost conceivable that a chocolate kiss could turn the night around.

"One last thing," the commandante said. He tossed a brown envelope to Ernesto, who contemptuously flung it down. A few photographs spilled out, along with an egg-shaped panty-hose container, which Clara pried open to reveal a gold watch, the familiar model of fake Rolex worn by Sonny, Ignacio, and don Lázaro.

A muffled sob shook Ernesto. All of a sudden he was surging toward me, eyes locked on mine. He grabbed my shoulders and slammed the top of his head into my face. Then he kneed me in the groin and clubbed the back of my neck.

I let myself fall. Curled up for protection, braced for the next blow, I fixed on a photograph of Sonny Tzoc's family posed in front of the Japanese Tea Garden in Golden Gate Park. I detected in their awkward stiffness, their tense smiles, a semblance of my own terror.

"Do you want the watch?" I heard the commandante say.

"I want to bury it in his mouth," Ernesto said.

"Not acceptable," the commandante said. "The watch is a resource of value."

When I moved my hands away from my face, they were red and wet with blood. I stared at them helplessly. Blood gushed from my nose. Someone, Clara, gave me a rag, the same rag Ernesto had used to clean his gun. I pressed it against my nose and leaned my head back. My temples throbbed.

"Let me shoot him," Ernesto said.

"Clara?" the commandante said.

I was staring straight up at the blue-black sky, velvety at the edges, hinting of the morning to come. Birds called to each other in the nearby trees. I must have had the opposite of an out-of-body experience—I had an *in*-body experience, so far *in* that even my sticky face seemed far away, and the sky, the enormous vault of sky, seemed infinitely distant.

"Life is sacred to us," Clara said. "It should never be wasted. We must ask what is to be gained from the death of this man."

"Satisfaction!" Ernesto said. "The pleasure of—"

"Let your *compañera* finish," the commandante said.

"Personal revenge is not a sufficient motive," Clara said. "The only reason to take a life is for the good of the people."

As she spoke, as I stanched the flow of blood from my nose and watched the sky inflate with light, I had an odd association—Clara sounded like an eager law school student trying to impress her professor—and this association, its particularity to me, inspired an overwhelming desire to survive.

"When I worked for the radio station," Clara was saying, "I met a young American volunteer, and she told me that up north no one has any idea what goes on in this country. They have no idea about the G-2 or the model villages or the bombs that burn the skin. She always emphasized publicity. 'The movement needs publicity.' 'A dead American is good for publicity. Especially a priest or nun,' is what she said. But perhaps a teacher is almost as good."

"Only if killed by the military," the young girl heating tortillas said. Men were lining up to be served. It was just breakfast time to them.

"Perhaps I disagree," Clara said. "Of course the military would deny killing him, but everyone knows how seldom they tell the truth."

In one fluid motion Ernesto slapped in the clip of his Kalachnikov, sighted my belly, and popped his lips apart.

"So you favor killing him?" the commandante asked Clara.

"I'm just articulating a position," she said.

"Counterpositions?" the commandante said.

"He has a face like my uncle," the tortilla girl said. "A good face."

"Very well," the commandante said. "Anything else?"

The fire crackled. Birds twittered in the trees. If the silence was intended to strain my nerves, it succeeded. No one looked at me except Ernesto while I folded and refolded the blood-soaked rag. My hands shook.

"Santiesteban," the commandante said. "What country did your parents come from?"

"Mexico," I said.

"Do you consider yourself a citizen of the United States?"

"Yes, sir."

The commandante lit a Marlboro and had the rest of the pack passed around. He seemed to be waiting for me to defend myself.

"Typical *yanqui* pig," Ernesto muttered. "He reeks of death."

"No!" I said. The word caught in my throat, but I rattled on, despite the hitch in my voice. "I was only doing a favor for my neighbor. That's the only reason I'm here. I have no antagonism toward you. We probably want the same things. I'm sympathetic. I don't know what more to say."

I found myself addressing Clara, as if she were my best hope. Her black eyes remained unfathomable.

"I'm not rich. I don't exploit anyone. I have no desire in the world for you people to be poor or hungry or oppressed by the military. I believe in education and goodwill and sharing."

I didn't think about truth. I didn't think about lying. I spoke only to reach Clara, but she cut me off. "Look at your jacket, your suitcase, your soap—"

"Excuse me," I said. "I wish you had all this too."

"Unfortunately, there are not enough gold watches to go around."

"The watch comes from Hong Kong," I said, as if that mattered.

"As long as the rich insist on gold watches, the poor will be left without enough to eat."

"I don't know," I said.

"Your neighbor, Santiago Tzoc, sent his brother a watch just like this one, well, it must have been years now. Sebastiano, of course, would never wear such an ostentatious object. It shined too much."

Ernesto clicked the safety of his Kalachnikov back and forth.

He muttered in a sullen monotone, "My father hid the watch at the bottom of his army trunk."

"Hidden or not, it became public knowledge," Clara said. "The fat one, Lázaro Muñoz, military commissioner of our district, offered a goat, a loom, and several chickens for the watch. He even agreed to settle a dispute over a small parcel of land."

Ernesto rested his forehead against the muzzle of his gun. "My father foresaw trouble—he was inclined to sacrifice the watch—but my mother and I said that if the fat one offered so much, it must be worth far more."

"The fat one denounced Sebastiano as a Communist," Clara said. "Sebastiano found out about the *calumnía,* but it would have cost four hundred quetzals to have his name removed from the list. The fat one was willing to loan him the money, but Sebastiano turned stubborn. The two of them had never gotten along.

"And then one day the *desconocidos* arrived in black ski masks and Sebastiano disappeared. His wife gave the watch to the fat one in order to secure his help, but it was too late. The body showed up, without much torture, in a ditch near Chebaj."

"And Ernesto joined the guerillas," I said, to prove that I was paying attention.

"Not yet," Clara said. "Sebastiano really had been helping our movement, and Ernesto had never approved. He took charge of his father's land and went on with his life, until a terrible mistake was made."

Ernesto stood up and I ducked. He circled the fire, gun in hand. Every time he passed behind me, I flinched.

"The radio station in Maluatla was accused of broadcasting Communist propaganda. One night soldiers in uniform appeared in town to interrogate those responsible. It so happened that the wife of Ernesto was also named Clara. She was interrogated instead of me."

"More than interrogated," Ernesto said.

"The wife was released next morning, unharmed."

"*La puta mierda!*" Ernesto said.

"Ernesto didn't believe her," Clara said.

Ernesto grabbed the front of my jacket and hauled me to my feet. "She lied to me," he said. I covered my nose. Yellow crumbs of tortilla sprayed up at my face as he sputtered. "If she had told the truth, I would have kept her, but she lied. 'Did they touch you?' I said. 'No,' she said. 'Did they molest you?' I said. 'Oh, no, Ernesto, they didn't touch me or molest me.' How could I keep a woman who would lie like that?"

He threw me down on top of the McDonald's coffee cup and the *Thriller* tape. The blood-caked rag I raised to my face was the color of dead leaves. Groping for my own handkerchief, I touched the canister of mace in my breast pocket. I wet the handkerchief with what little spit I could muster and tremulously scrubbed at the blood crusted under my nose.

The irrationality of Ernesto's story jacked up my fright. Nothing I could say would upset his illogic. Nothing I could do would prove my innocence.

It was the most beautiful dawn of my life. The emerging green of the trees seemed to promise eternal spring.

"I'm not responsible for your problems," I said to Ernesto, my impulse as irrational as any of his. "The blame is not mine. I have done nothing."

"You have done nothing," the commandante said, arching his back like a cat. "Is that your most persuasive argument?"

"My neighbor asked me for a favor. He wanted to share some of the things of his life in America with his family here in Guatemala. I was helping my neighbor. It's not fair to condemn me for that."

"It's not fair," the commandante repeated. "Tell me, please, what good are you alive?"

My nose started to bleed again. I got the hiccups. It occurred to me suddenly that this might be a test, a performance orchestrated to teach me, brainwash me, and if I gave the right answer I might pass. At the same time, I wondered if my answer mattered at all. It was like tiptoeing across a field that might or might not be mined.

"Life is sacred. Do unto others as you would have them do unto you. No one has the right to deprive anyone else of life."

Head tilted back, handkerchief to my nose, I tried to say something unstupid, but the commandante interrupted, his voice calm, almost gentle.

"Excuse me, but your country deprives my people of life every day. You train the government's forces to kill us more efficiently with bullets and bombs that you provide."

"My country shouldn't do that," I said. "But another dead body won't convince them not to. You need an advocate, a witness, to testify about what goes on here, the abuses of power. As a cadaver I'm worthless, but alive I can take your side. I can present your case to influential people."

"*Mierda,*" Ernesto said. "My own uncles are up north already. My own blood. Half of Guatemala is probably up there by now. If your country hasn't heard what's going on, it's not listening."

"Then there's no point to kill me for publicity," I said.

"I don't want to kill you for publicity," Ernesto said. "I want to kill you for revenge."

My hiccups stopped, but my nose kept bleeding. The commandante waved his hand at me as if I'd fallen behind and needed to catch up.

"As soon as I get back to California, I'm scheduled to speak to a group of very influential businessmen in my community. I'll tell them what I've seen. Believe me, I'll present your situation in the most sympathetic light. . . . We'll work to stop the sale of weapons, the human rights violations . . ."

The commandante was looking off at the trees, and so was everyone else, I realized. A spectacularly beautiful bird perched motionless on the highest branch of an aguacatillo tree not more than twenty feet from us. The bird stepped off the branch backwards, beating its wings like a huge woodpecker or hummingbird. It hovered in midair, snatching lime-green aguacatillo fruits with quick thrusts of its beak. The bird's tail must have been three feet long. In the thin light of dawn, it gave off a dark green iridescent shimmer more dazzling than the jewels of a peacock. And then the bird suddenly rose, calling *weep weep weep weep weep weep* and swooped above the trees, soaring over our end of the soccer field for many seconds before it drifted up the hill and fluttered down somewhere out of sight.

The tortilla girl served the commandante last. He used the Frisbee as a plate. Clara sorted through the rest of my belongings, my former belongings, dividing them into piles, things to keep and things to throw away. The soap she slipped into her own pocket and buttoned the flap. When she wavered over the chocolate kisses, I heard myself plead: "May I? May I please?"

"Why not?" the commandante said.

The plastic bag refused to yield to my clumsy fingers. Frustrated, I bit off a corner, shook out an avalanche of kisses, scratched the foil off one, and popped it into my mouth. Sucking the sweet chocolate, I felt for the first time that I held everybody's attention.

"My neighbor Santiago enjoys these very much," I said. "I know he wished that his family would enjoy them too."

"I will try one," the commandante said, as if to prove his courage to any skeptics. He swallowed the kiss whole, like a pill, and looked around the fire at each of his followers. "Any more requests?"

I clasped my hands behind my head. My will had ebbed, or my adrenaline. I thought of a magazine article I'd read at Spoon's parents' house about the last words of airline pilots before they crashed. I'd expected that the most common last word would be something like *Jesus* or *mother,* but the most common last word turned out to be *shit.* I was no longer surprised.

Men rolled up their gear inside their blankets. The tortilla girl unplugged a vacuum tube from an ancient radio, thumped it, spit on it, and put it back. Clara leafed through my Rilke book.

"I do have another request," I said. "May I write a short letter to my mother in Reedley?"

Let me confess right now that the letter was strictly an excuse to mention my mother, to invoke the love between mother and son, a desperate attempt by a shameless man to convince anyone who might be sympathetic that I deserved to live.

"Reedley?" the commandante said. "I know Reedley. King's

River. Del Monte Packing Plant. I picked grapes and nectarines in the Bracero program."

"I grew up in Reedley," I said. "My mother lives right near Pioneer Park."

"Yes, yes, yes." The commandante grinned like an impish boy. I kept my father's prejudice against the braceros to myself.

"Why don't you kiss him?" Ernesto said to the commandante. "Let's roast a chicken for our honored guest."

"Please, Ernesto," Clara said. "The movement is not served by personal discourse."

"Everything is personal," the commandante said. "To forget this is to forget why we fight." The commandante tapped the Frisbee like a tambourine. His little finger was just a stump, I noticed with a start. "I was not inclined to execute this *norteamericano* in the first place—"

"You never are," Ernesto said.

"That's because I remember why I'm here. You still haven't learned. You love only hatred and violence. No, it's not love exactly. You are a fish, and violence is the river you swim in."

"If I can't kill him, I want him to lick my boots," Ernesto said.

"When I was a little boy in the capital," the commandante said, "my family listened to Franklin Roosevelt on the radio, the whole family, even the maid, because my father was progressive in those things. My father taught the speeches of Franklin Roosevelt in his classes at the university. The four freedoms. You wouldn't remember. The United States was a great country then, and even when I picked grapes and nectarines there it had a bit of generosity left, but now it is truly an octopus, and no one remembers the noble ideas except a few old fools."

"I want him to lick my boots," Ernesto said again.

I didn't wait for an argument. I got down on my knees and kissed each boot.

"Lick them," Ernesto said. "Lick them clean."

The boots tasted of chalk and clay and gunpowder.

"My father wore these boots," Ernesto said.

Bent low and licking, strangely at ease, I remembered how I'd bowed to Spoon the night of my thirtieth birthday. My mind skipped from his cheery flip-flops to the hard black shoes my father had worn even to the beach . . .

"Now the other one," Ernesto said.

The sun must have cleared the far end of the field, because I saw shadows, elongated shadows even skinnier than the human beings who cast them. Then the shadows shifted.

I'd like to believe that it was Clara who hit me.

I'd like to believe that it was Clara who spared me a harder blow.

XI

ORTHOPEDIC SHOES

Things go better with Coke.
CAPITALIST JINGLE

Dateline: La Esperanza. This just in from election central. (I promise I'll be brief. Mercifully brief.) Picture me sitting at the foreman's rolltop desk in the pleasant shade under the bola tree. Yes, the same bola tree where only the night before I'd sunk to my knees and pleaded without dignity for a morsel of affection. Today, on this warm and hazy morning, it seemed inconceivable to have exerted so much energy, not to mention emotion. A lazy breeze rustled the dry leaves, the radio on the porch played a slow tearjerker, we passed the time chatting and eating sunflower seeds.

Most of the resident workers had already voted. They'd lined up as soon as the polls had opened. Correction: as soon as the *poll* had opened—there was only one voting booth, a rusty portable outhouse which had stood unused, as far as we could tell, since the fall of the Mayan empire. In the first cool hour after dawn, nearly a hundred men, women, and children had marked their ballots and dropped them into the oil drum next to my desk. It was a clever setup, if I do say so myself, and of course I do. Each of the three candidates wore a makeshift sandwich billboard inscribed with a symbol. Hércules wore a quetzal, Tomás wore an ear of corn, the houseboy Memín wore a pyramid. The same symbols (plus an extra) appeared on the ballots, which I'd photocopied in Sololá. Refugio had done all the artwork with a magic marker. Democracy in action. My finest hour. Now we waited in the gathering heat to see who else would show up, if anyone.

"Man proposes, God disposes," Tomás was saying to Hércules.

"In our case it's don Hoover who disposes," Hércules said.

"If we treat don Hoover as the devil, he will surely grow horns," Tomás said. "What we need is his goodwill."

Two women straggled down the path from the workers' quarters. One of them shyly explained in Tzutzil that they hadn't voted yet because they'd been busy in the kitchen. Tomás translated. (There are eighteen different Indian languages in Guatemala—eighteen different obstacles to organization.) The women wanted to go into the voting booth together—what is it about women and bathrooms?—but I staunchly defended the sanctity of the secret ballot. They crossed themselves and spoke of snakes lurking under the floorboards. I put aside my electoral scruples. *Power to the people*—that's my motto. It was the fact of the election that mattered, not the form.

Refugio scooped a hatful of sunflower seeds out of the sack on my desk and offered some to Tomás, who bowed in thanks, crinkling his sandwich billboard. Refugio returned the bow. Soon they were bowing comically back and forth. Hércules shaded his eyes as if Refugio's bald spot was blinding him. Refugio, in retaliation, imitated Hércules ardently combing his hair. Even the foreman, watching from the porch with his AK-47, allowed himself a smile. He ordered the houseboy to make lemonade.

We were comfortable in the shade under the bola tree. The heat was like a warm bath. If I hadn't banned liquor from the polling area, I would have found a bottle to pass around.

When the Indian women emerged from the outhouse, they proudly displayed their ballots folded to postage-stamp size. "Secret," they said. "Very secret."

"Long live the Magna Carta," I said.

And then we heard the distant burst of a sputtering engine. My first thought was thugs sent by Hoover to disrupt the election. A black cloud of exhaust crested the hill, followed by a shortbed truck. With all due machismo I spit out a gob of mushy sunflower-seed husks. Benigno checked the clip on his AK-47. All of us seemed to gravitate toward the road.

If I'm building this up too much, it's because I was ready for a classic confrontation. High noon at La Esperanza. So what if Hércules and Tomás looked like Alice in Wonderland rejects?

We had just the right mix of drama and farce. Our hero — *me,* Macho McGuffin — would defend democracy against the forces of evil. That the forces of evil turned out to be the forces of good, or of not-so-bad, was not my fault.

Chongo Espada, the mechanic Armando had seen me talking to in Sololá, had hauled down an overflow cargo of *jornaleros,* seasonal workers, all of whom expected to reap the benefits of the democratic process. The first man to dislodge himself from the sweltering hold of the truck asked me in a sly whisper if they would truly get paid to vote for Hércules. What could I say? The foreman was making me nervous, circling around to keep everyone in his sights. I definitely understood why politicians prefer to do business in back rooms.

Chongo Espada pumped my hand. "You see?" he shouted to the men. "Just as I promised."

"Which is Hércules?" one of them asked.

"I'm afraid we have a problem," I said for all to hear. I announced in my eloquent way that I couldn't pay anyone to vote, particularly not for a specific candidate.

Chongo protested. Hadn't I assured him only yesterday that a vote was worth plenty? Weren't these men sacrificing a full day's wages in order to participate in *my* election? Who would cover the expenses — food, gasoline, wear and tear on his truck? Once I saw Chongo's angle, I let him talk me into a compromise. All the men would receive travel money, whether they voted or not. I emphasized that voting was voluntary, that votes must be freely cast for the candidate of choice. In the interest of an informed electorate, I invited Hércules and Tomás to say a few words, but the foreman interrupted, his voice high and pinched: "This is not regular."

"What's regular?" I said. "Show me the rules. There are no rules. We invent the rules as we go along."

The foreman's pained expression didn't change much. I think he wore tight underwear. "How do you know these men have worked here?"

"I'll ask them," I said.

"Make them present proof. Make them show pay stubs."

"Benigno, Benigno. I'm truly pleased at your concern. And

I appreciate your advice even if I don't follow it in this case."

"Don Marlón would never—"

"Don Marlón is elsewhere. Praise the Lord."

The foreman held the only gun, but he didn't flaunt it. He was professional enough not to aim his gun unless he meant to shoot. He exacted a milder form of revenge though. When the houseboy dared to venture back with the pitcher of lemonade, the foreman dumped it out.

Otherwise, Chongo's men voted without further incident. They talked to the candidates and ate sunflower seeds. Hércules pledged his commitment to health first and money second. He called for affordable medicine in the company store and a ban on the pesticide *ganiexcan*. Tomás stressed the need for patience and a good attitude. Both of them said that Chongo should put benches in his truck and only carry as many passengers as would fit on the benches. They fielded questions about higher wages, lower prices, better food.

After the men re-sardined themselves into the truck and headed up the road wreathed in black smoke, Hércules and Tomás kept talking. The hottest part of the day stretched out ahead of us. I put my feet on the desk and tilted back my chair. I had a modest feeling of accomplishment—if any feeling of mine was ever modest. I wondered what it would be like to run the *finca*. I wondered if I could do a few decent people some good. And then I wondered if Hoover had set me up for this sentiment.

Of course I couldn't help thinking about Magdalena. She was so different from any other woman I'd been involved with. So old fashioned. I longed to make her forget her scruples in a frenzy of ecstatic bliss. Delusions of sexual grandeur? Let's just say I had confidence in my powers of carnal persuasion.

Hours later, the only other voters would drive down from Santa Catalina in a borrowed school bus. They would bring *aguardiente* and a *marimba*, the resident workers would provide a benedictory chunk of goat meat, and together we would celebrate the election.

But I prefer to remember the time in between, the long afternoon ebb when the air grew heavy and even the birds snoozed. Only Hércules and Tomás had energy. They talked and talked. They actually considered each other's ideas. And Refugio, my wise friend Refugio, after passing around yet another hatful of sunflower seeds, stifled a monstrous yawn and said, "It's good to see that a man's head is not just for wearing hats."

Which reminds me that in the land of the free and the home of the brain-dead we don't even use our heads for that.

The quiet in my office now is the opposite of that afternoon quiet—insomniac instead of sleepy, empty instead of full. I hear the ominous hum of my mini-refrigerator. I hear the janitor out in the hallway. The soles of his orthopedic shoes squish against the vinyl tile. *Squish-squeak. Squish-squeak.* I open a can of Diet Coke. My third so far tonight. The aluminum rips. The bubbles hiss. I fill the can to overflowing with Puerto Rican rum. *Gurgle-glug. Gurgle-glug.*

Did I promise to be brief?

I need to put on my Walkman and crank up the volume.

(I wish I could type without hearing each word vibrate inside my head.)

XII

FEVER DREAM

La vida es sueño.

CALDERON DE LA BARCA

Consciousness returned as the drone of mosquitoes and the buzz of flies.

Light tingle on the back of the neck, a sting, the attempt to touch it, and the discovery that I couldn't move, not without an impossible effort.

There's a difference between the drone of mosquitoes and the buzz of flies. It's remarkably easy to hear when you have nothing to do but listen.

Pain emanated from every brain cell, the gray matter, the white matter, the skull itself. Am I being melodramatic? The pain intertwined with the buzz of flies and the drone of mosquitoes like a chord from a Gothic organ that drowned out every other sound, every other sensation. Yes, I am being melodramatic.

My head hurt. My brain didn't work right. Flies and mosquitoes mauled me.

Gradually, though, my zone of awareness expanded. I realized that there was something loose in my mouth, something as hard as teeth but larger. My arms were pinned under my heavy body. I smelled excrement.

When I tried to lift my head, it threatened to shatter. Waves of pain radiated into the air around me, beyond my physical boundaries, like the ache of phantom limbs. Spoon's mother might have said that my aura hurt.

I lay facedown and breathed, just breathed, for quite awhile. My nose was plugged with blood and mucus. The sharp-edged object in my mouth was wrapped around my tongue so tight that I couldn't spit it out. I opened my eyes and saw brown clots of dirt, yellow stalks of dry grass, a trail of red ants angling toward the corner of a burlap sack. I wondered how many

Guatemalans had woken up in this position. I wondered how many Guatemalans in this position had woken up. I thought of Sebastiano Tzoc, his body found in a ditch near Chebaj, "without much torture." The body of Armando Santiesteban was lying in a pile of excrement, but at least the chest of Armando Santiesteban still heaved up and down. At least the heart still pumped.

With a minimum of jarring motion, I wriggled my right arm out from under me, then my left, then I worked them nearer and nearer my head, which thrummed like an overheated amp. The watch, as I untwisted it, scraped the taste buds off my tongue. I imagined the joke Spoon would make about my new mouthwatch. Despite the sticky dent in my skull and the blood crusted to my hair, I felt high-spirited. A silly tune I couldn't quite place eluded my moribund memory. I didn't even particularly like the tune, but I had to remember where I'd heard it. And then it came to me:

> *Jesus gives me freedom*
> *Freedom*
> *Freedom*
> *Jesus gives me freedom*
> *No one will ever take from me.*

I croaked out a few notes, but my voice sounded broken, so I stopped. As I nestled my head in the crook of my arms, I had a foolish thought: *at least things couldn't get worse.*

When I was seven or eight years old, before I started my own paper route, I helped a friend with his. One wet winter day, the banner headline in the afternoon paper said: "RUSSIANS PERFECT DOOMSDAY DEVICE." Neither of us understood exactly what that meant, but we fretted about it while we pedaled along Manning Street in the rain. Later, at dinner, I asked my mother for an explanation. She said that the Russians were people just like us who loved their families very much. My father was always suspicious of conversation, especially at the table, but he narrowed his eyes and got that melancholy smirk of his. He poured salt into his can of Budweiser and squeezed in half a lime. "I'll tell you what it means, *mi hijo*," he said. "It means that any time, even right now, some *pendejo* with a hangover can push one button and blow us human beans to kingdom come." I caught the flu that night and dreamed of the doomsday device, an endless series of explosions, bomb after bomb lighting the entire world on fire, luminous scraps of bodies, buildings, machines all falling in the dark, falling and falling, until, after the debris had finally settled, weird, humanesque plants began to grow from the glowing earth. Most of my fever dreams since then have been more or less the same, with variations: in this case mules, mine fields, the shoes of Ernesto Tzoc.

I lay sweaty and shivering in the yellow grass, half-awake, half-asleep, until a burst of gunfire ruptured my trance. I had no idea whether the shots had been fired anywhere near me. I didn't know if I was out in the open or hidden from view. I kept still, listening, hoping to be left alone.

A voice spoke at such close range that I heard not only the words but the moist click of tongue against teeth.

"Kill him," the voice said.

"First make sure he's dead," a second voice said.

I was afraid to move and afraid not to move. I did the most unthreatening thing I could think of: I sang the Jesus song, *Jesus gives me freedom,* an entire verse, before I turned over and looked up.

The barrel of an automatic rifle pointed at me, blinding in the glare. I shaded my eyes and tried to orient myself. I lay in a clump of weeds and short grass at the base of a steep hill. A rocky field stretched out beyond the pair of jittery soldiers, who seemed to regard me as dangerous, a maniac who might be hiding a grenade.

"Get up, man. Or are you a toad?"

"I'm an American citizen," I said.

"Of course. And we are gauchos from the pampas."

A spray of shots kicked up dust right in front of me. I swayed to my feet. The nausea was even worse than the headache. To steady myself, I looked off into the distance and happened to see the goalposts at the far end of the field. The guerillas' fire pit smoldered less than a dozen steps away.

"I'm an American," I said, first in English and then in Spanish with an exaggerated gringo accent. "Look at my—"

I intended to indicate my Goretex jacket or my Samsonite suitcase or my Hush Puppies, but they were gone. I pulled out my pockets—no passport, no wallet, no American change. "Wait!" I said. Gingerly, I reached down for the burlap sack, which yielded a pack of Kools, the Frisbee, and five chocolate kisses. I stood before the soldiers barefoot, excrement smeared on my pants, my nose broken, my face caked with blood. "This is American," I said. "This is a Frisbee. My neighbor in the United States asked me to bring it to his family here in Guatemala. You throw it, see? It's a toy, an American toy. Like this, see?" I drew back my arm; the soldiers tensed; the Frisbee wobbled, fluttered, and fell at their boots. If my survival depended on throwing the Frisbee like a true American, I was dead. "Believe me, I'm a visitor in your country. The victim of a misunderstanding."

Two groups of soldiers who must have been circling the field in opposite directions now converged on us.

"Lieutenant, we found a man without papers," my chief tormentor said. "He sings like a sick frog."

The lieutenant dispatched one group to search the campfire area and the other to cover the hill. He was a handsome man about my age, with laugh lines around his eyes and good teeth.

"How is it that you find yourself here?" he said.

"I come from California," I said. "I'm an American citizen. My best friend is marrying the daughter of don Hoover Schultz—do you know him?"

The lieutenant shook his head. Unfortunately, Hoover's sphere of influence didn't stretch this far.

"A neighbor of mine, a Guatemalan, asked me to deliver a package to his brother, who lives—or used to live—in Maluatla. Unfortunately, some guerillas—I suppose they were guerillas—sort of abducted me, and then I woke up here."

"How many guerillas?" the lieutenant said. He exuded competence, like a bright young doctor. I wanted to trust him, but I couldn't.

"I don't know," I said. "I didn't see much. I was blindfolded the whole time."

"You didn't see much or you didn't see anything?"

"I saw nothing."

"What did you hear?"

"Well, there was one they called *Commandante*. He was the leader. The others were called *compañero*."

"How enlightening," the lieutenant said. He drank from his canteen. I was very thirsty. "And what was in the package?" he asked, licking his wet lips.

"Lots of things. American things. That Frisbee. A coffee cup. Family pictures. Cigarettes."

"Excuse me. You saw those things? Or else you heard very detailed exclamations."

"I saw the things, well, my friend and I peeked in the package back in California. We shouldn't have."

"Lieutenant, this man had no blindfold when we found him." The soldier cackled just like a kid I'd known in high school, a kid who'd once bragged about an experiment he'd conducted with a firecracker and a cat.

"My private is suspicious," the lieutenant said. "You have been among guerillas and yet here you are alive. Why should they spare you? At certain times and places, to be alive is a sign of guilt."

"I'm neutral," I said. Without thinking, I clutched my father's cross.

The lieutenant simply waited for a better answer. I did my best to outwait him. We watched the private play with the Frisbee, angling it up into the breeze so that it would glide back to him. A few thin clouds formed on the horizon. The heat intensified. Suddenly, the private braced his gun against his thigh and fired away at the Frisbee. My feet splayed out from under me. The lieutenant touched my shoulder and I crumpled to my knees.

"Don't shoot me," I said. "I'm worth more to you alive than dead. Listen, I can be your witness. I can plead your case to the people of the United States. My sympathies—" I happened to notice the fake Rolex glittering nearby in the yellow grass. The crystal was cracked but unclouded. "Here! Look! This is evidence for your investigation. Take it. Take it. It came in the package. The guerillas must have left it behind."

I held out the watch in the palm of my hand. If it had been a poison apple or a cleverly disguised bomb, I would have urged it on the lieutenant just as fervently.

He slipped on the fake Rolex next to his own watch. "Lázaro Muñoz is a very vigilant military commissioner. I have to file a report on this incident, not that I wish to detain you for lengthy questioning, but . . ."

"Please," I said. "I need to return to the capital for my friend's wedding."

"Suppose your blindfold had slipped," the lieutenant said. "How many guerillas do you imagine you would have seen? Remember, everything you tell me is already known."

"Maybe twelve. Maybe fifteen."

"And judging by the commandante's voice, what might he look like?"

"Old and small and mole-ish, with the darkest eyes."

"And the others?"

"A tall thin woman with a bowl haircut and a jagged scar on her right wrist. A wild beast of a man. I believe they had an old radio with vacuum tubes. . . . Oh, yes, the commandante's little finger was missing. The woman's name was Clara. . . ."

The lieutenant listened tactfully; inquired about weapons, supplies, uniforms. I sipped water from his canteen and informed on the guerillas while the corporal used the Frisbee for target practice.

"How did they strike you as people?" the lieutenant finally asked. "Ready to quit? Defiant? Would you call them truly evil or simply misguided?"

I didn't know what answer the lieutenant wanted. "It's not a normal situation they're in," I said.

"I often speculate," the lieutenant said. "They cross a line, and once they cross it, they have nothing to believe in except destruction. That's the difference you should understand. The army is far from perfect, but at least we believe in a stable country and a stable family."

"I'll try to remember that," I said, staring at his heavy black boots, better polished than Ernesto's, but otherwise similar.

Gently, with one finger, he lifted my chin. "Don't be ashamed of your survival instinct. It serves one well in this country."

I scrutinized his face for a sign of disgust or contempt; listened to his voice for a note of mockery. I wondered how many times in his short career he'd killed or ordered killing. And yet he seemed compassionate. His gold wedding band sparkled, his new watch gleamed as he filled out several stencilled forms, including a letter of transit and a receipt for the cigarettes, which he apologetically confiscated. I didn't care. I just wanted to be alone with the chocolate kisses.

The lieutenant thwarted my plans, though. He ordered the private who'd blasted the Frisbee to ensure my safe return to Guatemala City.

The private behaved himself until we were well along the path to Maluatla, but then he started poking me from behind with the muzzle of his gun. Thorns and sharp stones cut my bare feet. When I had to slow down, he thrust the gun barrel between my legs.

"How do you like it?" he said.

The sensation of his breath on the back of my neck made me shiver.

"Probably about as much as you would like it," I said. "Or maybe even less."

"What do you mean by that?" he said.

I still had the mace in my breast pocket, and I decided to use it if all else failed. "Do you know California?" I said. "Disneyland? Hollywood? Fernando Valenzuela?"

"Have you ever gutted a wild pig?" he said.

I clenched my hands into fists. "Why are you doing this to me?" I said. I was trying to sound tough, but I sounded pathetic. An uncontrollable spasm shook me from the inside out. Tears welled up. *If he sees me cry, he'll kill me,* I thought, but my defenses stifled only the first few sobs. I cried as quietly as possible.

"Shut up," the corporal said.

It was beyond my power to explain that it was beyond my power to stop.

"Just walk," he said. He began muttering scraps of violence and jabbing me with the gun. "Butcher the pig," he grunted, stabbing the gun barrel between my shoulder blades. "Cut out the guts and drain the blood." He spoke as if I couldn't hear, as if I were already dead.

I cried most of the way to Maluatla, where we joined the road to Chebaj, the new road, not the overgrown mule path I'd trodden less than twenty-four hours before. The pavement improved my pace. At the bridge outside Chebaj, the corporal waved down a truck hauling onions to Guatemala City and slapped me on the rear as I climbed into the passenger seat.

I sneaked my chocolate kisses a nibble at a time. To share seemed hypocritical for a man with no virtue. I fell asleep slumped against the vibrating door and dreamed of food: corn and squash at Refugio's house, mushrooms almandine at Casa Schultz, the little yellow cakes on the silver tray under the bola tree at La Esperanza.

The longest day of my life was more than half over.

XIII

GRIEF

*... and when something weird happens, when you
find a spider in your shoe or if you take a breath
and feel like a broken window, then you have to
tell what's happening, tell it to the guys at the
office or to the doctor. Oh, doctor, every time I
take a breath ... Always tell it, always get rid
of that tickle in the stomach that bothers you.*

JULIO CORTÁZAR

I woke up with my mouth open and drool on my chin. The
truck had stopped. The idling engine coughed and sputtered. It
was after dark.

"How do you feel?" the driver said. I heard him spit.

"Where are we?" I asked. The grainy light of the high beams
illuminated nothing.

"Guatemala," he said.

"Where in Guatemala?" I said.

"Right here in the heart of the capital. Do you feel well?"

"Very well," I answered automatically. I didn't want to analyze my discomfort, but I was aware that certain parts of my
body hurt more than others.

He reached across my lap and unhooked the thin wire holding the door shut, the door I'd leaned my full weight against for
several hours.

"Is this a good place to get out?" I said.

"The best," he said.

"Pray for me," I said as I stepped down from the cab.

How do you compare fear of death to fear of embarrassment? I
was seriously worried. In front of me stretched a long row of
unlighted stalls, entirely deserted in both directions. I didn't
know where I was. I didn't know where Casa Schultz was. I had
no money, no passport, no shoes. As I fingered my father's

cross, the truck brayed like a lovesick mule and pulled away, revealing, as I turned to wave, a line of motley taxis parked across the street, several drivers pitching coins at the curb. I still had no money, but I didn't need to tell them that. Wasn't I an American? Wasn't I entitled to certain eccentricities?

I swaggered into the middle of their *fútbol* debate and demanded to be taken to Goya Street.

"Yes, sir. Snappy, snappy."

In the backseat of a Ford Pinto, my smell caught up with me. I decided that as soon as we got to Casa Shultz, I'd run for the shower and leave the doorman and the taxi driver to sort things out.

"Sl-o-o-ow," I said as we turned onto Avenida Goya.

We seemed to be heading in the right direction. Armed guards patrolled the driveways. High walls separated the mansions from the shacks. Luckily, it was impossible to miss the barbed wire laced with twinkling Christmas lights on the block before Casa Schultz.

"Ah-KEY, ah-KEY," I said.

I bolted from the taxi as planned, but the old doorman refused to open the front door. Instead, with an expression worthy of the most refined butler, he sniffed. The taxi driver scratched his belly button through a tear in his T-shirt. A dog barked, and then Magdalena's rich contralto sang over the static of the intercom: "What is it, Pepito?"

"Magdalena," I said. "It's Armando Santiesteban. The best man. I'm sorry to bother you like this. I ran into trouble. But don't worry," I continued as the door swung open. "Patricio wasn't with me. I'm sure he's fine."

Magdalena was holding a paperback in her hand, her index finger marking her place. When she saw me, she covered her mouth with the book. Her dark cheeks flushed darker. Aunt Martha growled at her side.

"Please excuse my terrible appearance," I said.

She squeezed my arm. I might have given her a hug if I hadn't smelled so bad.

"He's a friend, Aunt Martha. Come in. Come in."

The taxi driver coughed politely. I pulled out my empty

pockets. Magdalena carried no money in her baggy sweat suit, but Pepito promised to settle the fare. I doubt if he tipped.

In the swank downstairs bathroom, Magdalena and I petted Aunt Martha while the long lavender tub slowly filled with steamy water.

"You don't mind a little bubble bath?" she said.

"Bubble bath is fine."

"If it wouldn't bother you, I could go into your room and get fresh clothes?"

"That would be fantastic," I said. "I never want to see these again."

"Are you starving? Shall I heat some soup?"

"Wonderful," I said.

She sat on the rim of the bathtub with her slim legs crossed at the knees. Her black helmet of hair shined in the soft light as she bent down to rub Aunt Martha's stomach. "I've been very worried tonight," she said.

"This has been the longest day of my life," I said. "I was almost shot."

"It's over now," she said. "You don't have to talk."

The pleasure of stripping away each of my foul shirts, peeling off my gross jeans in the clean steam of the bathroom almost made up for the whole ordeal, or so it seemed until a hideous black bug with pincers and sinister antennae crawled from the heap of clothes and scuttled across the purple throw rug. Naked, I snatched it up in one of the T-shirts and flushed it down the toilet, but not before it delivered its deflating message: *You may be in the lap of luxury now, boy, but don't forget that you were really out there. Don't forget how it really is.*

Magdalena served me in Hoover's study. My appetite was less hearty than I expected. I managed only a bite of cheese sandwich, a swallow of beer, and a few spoonfuls of thin soup. Magdalena hovered over me, swabbing my head wound with disinfectant while my swollen feet soaked in a Montenegro family healing potion.

"It all started with a Rolex," I said.

"Hold still," Magdalena said. She pressed my head against her flat stomach. Something hard in the pouch of her sweatshirt dug into both of us—the laughable canister of mace. "Oh," she said. "I found this in one of your pockets."

"My birthday gift from my mother. What a joke."

"If it was a gift, you should keep it." She poured Mercurochrome on another cotton swab and aimed a final dab at my battered skull.

"Thanks for taking care of me," I said.

"You're a good patient," she said. "I feel very comfortable with you. Sometimes with Patricio I don't know how to behave."

When she sank down beside me on the black leather couch, I didn't know how to behave either. Wedding paraphernalia cluttered the coffee table—travel brochures, checklists, swatches of fabric, a pamphlet from the Church of the Most Precious Blood.

"Aren't you hungry?" she said.

"I guess not." I stared at the coffee table. "So wait'll you hear what happened."

"Just relax," she said. "Give me your feet."

"I can't relax until I get this story out of my system."

"Please, Armando, the brutality in my country sickens me too much."

"I'm sorry," I said. I lay down on the couch and she dried my puffy feet with a soft towel. "Let me tell you something else, then. I remembered some strange stuff this afternoon."

My feet were dry, but she kept on rubbing them through the towel. I talked in order not to swoon.

"I used to steal when I was a kid. All my friends stole candy and sodas, but I stole paperback books. One Saturday afternoon at this grocery store called Piggly Wiggly, I twirled the book rack for twenty minutes and then I bought a Big Hunk and a Mars bar. That was part of my clever strategy, to actually pay for something, but it didn't work. The manager stopped me just outside the automatic doors and made me open my viola case, which was empty except for *Tortilla Flat* by John Steinbeck and *The Yogi Berra Story*."

"Do you play the viola?" Magdalena asked.

"Not since junior high. But the case was perfect for stealing, or so I believed until I got caught."

Magdalena painted the cuts on my feet with Mercurochrome, which tickled more than it stung.

"At first I claimed total innocence —'How should I know where the books came from? Maybe my little brother hid them in there' — but the manager wasn't stupid. He was an old Armenian guy with white hair growing out of his ears. He said we were going to call my parents. I told him I was sorry. He dragged me over to the telephone and I started to cry. I cried louder and louder while he looked up our number and dialed. I cried hysterically. 'Please,' I begged him. 'If you hang up now, I promise I'll never steal again.' 'I'm supposed to trust the word of a thief?' he said. 'I'm not a thief. I'm a kid.' I was indignant that he didn't trust me. My little brother answered the phone, we both heard his small voice, and the manager dramatically hung up. 'If you break your word,' he said, 'not only will God punish you, but I personally will knock your block off.'"

"Knock your block off?" Magdalena said.

"On the way home I vowed never to cry again. The very next night I started counting the number of days in a row I hadn't cried. I called them *perfect days*. The total must have reached five or six hundred before I lost count. And years later, when I dropped out of law school and my father died and I split up with my wife, I couldn't cry. I couldn't even cry at my father's funeral. I knew it would be good for me, but I couldn't make myself do it."

Magdalena leaned over and squeezed my hand. We held that off-balance position for several seconds, until Aunt Martha growled and Spoon appeared in the doorway, his face as sickly white as skim milk, his pale blue eyes huge.

XIII

GRIEF *(interrupted)*

Forgive me for barging in like this. No, sincerely, I mean it. On the whole I'd rather be in Philadelphia. But here I am, under the influence of six diet *Cuba Libres*, the queen of the blues wailing in my ears, and my fingers have a life of their own. (It ain't a good life, but it's their life, *comprende?*)

Which brings me to the night in question. (For the record, Your Honor, I'm deleting Armando's account of the post-election debacle because it was based strictly on hearsay—he only knew what I told him and I didn't tell him much.)

Refugio and I counted votes on the porch of the hacienda. Refugio reached deep into the oil drum for each ballot, which he ceremoniously unfolded and handed over with a flourish. I marked my ledger under the name of the appropriate candidate and tore the ballot in half. It was a pleasant duty, except for the battle of the bands. The foreman's radio was blaring the latest Latin elevator music loud enough to drown out the marimba being played by three hip Santa Catalina dudes under the spreading bola tree. Why do other countries get the worst of U.S. culture? The deadly pesticides, the defective machinery, the muzak? Muzak is to real music as embalming fluid is to blood. But enough glib gab. Tomás received 84 votes, Hércules 67, Memín 9. And the extra symbol, the *huípil*, received 2.

I announced the results from the porch steps. The workers whistled for Tomás, who shuffled up the stairs and waved his hat.

"I am no one special," he said. "I need your help."

He called to Hércules to join him. Everyone quieted down. Hércules didn't shuffle up the stairs—he ascended with the dignity of a pope. When Tomás extended his hand, Hércules hesitated for a second. He looked Tomás over as if he could x-ray his soul.

"I voted late this afternoon," Hércules said, "not for myself but for this man. He promises no miracles, but he commands respect."

Tomás shyly thanked him and everyone else, including don Hoover, and I declared the results official.

"Long live democracy," I said, and all of a sudden I felt a terrible letdown. I'd heard something in my voice—sarcasm or derision—and my half-assed attitude seemed criminal. I sat heavily on the creaky steps. Hércules and Refugio sat beside me.

"What a relief," Hércules said.

"Well done," Refugio said.

"I'm just starting to think it was a joke," I said.

"No more than any other thing," Hércules said. "I myself am pleased with the results."

"Really?" I said.

"Tomás lives here," Hércules said. "He has the ear of the *patrón*. And consider this—when he finally raises his voice, it won't be dismissed as the voice of a troublemaker. Not that I'm a troublemaker. Despite my reputation. I only make trouble for the widow."

"She lives for your trouble," Refugio said.

"Perhaps," Hércules said. "My life is a disaster, isn't it? I need to tend my own *milpa* for awhile."

"But what about the election?" I said. "You have hope for these people?"

"They'll work until they die," Hércules said. "That they'll suffer we cannot doubt. But I remember what you said the other day. Even the illusion of change is better than no change at all."

"Did I say that? I don't always believe what I say."

"You convinced me," Hércules said. "And if you convinced me with words you didn't believe, then maybe you'll convince a poor soul or two with this election."

Refugio slapped us both on the back. "Look how many Indians have eaten goat meat tonight. One of La Esperanza's own goats, if I'm not mistaken. I'm going to celebrate with a piss."

Hércules and I stayed put. It was the perfect opportunity to thank him, and I had plenty to thank him for, but I just stared at a knothole the shape of Africa on the bottom step.

"I'm going to celebrate myself," he finally said.

I knew what he meant, but I should have asked him why he wouldn't use a word like *piss*. It occurred to me that he was striving to be refined—unlike Armando, an honest-to-God prude. I thought of Armando while the radio blasted a commercial for a new candy bar. The ultimate achievement of Western civilization. I wondered if somehow this poor sop of an election could possibly have been worthwhile. Maybe it was so ridiculous it made sense.

And then a burst of gunfire ended my speculation.

It sounded almost like firecrackers. "Eat the best," the smooth voice on the radio said.

I bolted toward the shots, toward where Hércules had headed, the banana trees that edged the road.

Not that I deserve a medal, but I wasn't afraid. I ran straight, out in the open, lit by the moon. I glanced under every banana tree, scanned the rows of coffee shrubs.

A glimpse of white dropped me into a crouch. Hércules lay inert, fallen over a coffee shrub, his body twisted, his white shirt and white pants dotted with dark smears. He'd pulled his knife halfway out of the scabbard buckled to his wrist, I saw when I turned him over. He'd pissed on himself.

I put my ear to his chest. All I heard was the insignificant noise of Benigno's radio.

Refugio called my name—as if I was in charge, as if I would know what to do.

Far up the hill a motorcycle sputtered into gear, a motorcycle with a broken muffler.

I don't remember unbuckling Hércules' knife or groping in his pockets for the keys to his truck, but I swear that as soon as I heard the motorcycle I started running. I already held the keys in my bloody hand. And the knife was already buckled to my wrist.

Armando, in his gutless version, refused to pass judgment, as if there might be any doubt who committed the murder. There was no doubt. The motorcycle with the broken muffler belonged to Marlón. Not the foreman. Not the corporal from Santa Catalina.

I drove under the influence of an elaborate fantasy—that I could save Hércules just by driving faster. A little more speed and I'd get to a place where Hércules wasn't dead yet, a place just up the road, or just down the brain, a node, a junction where the news hadn't reached. As I skidded into each turn and hit the gas, I felt as though I was racing against Hércules' death and losing. I stuck my head out the window and screamed: "Fuck. Fuck. Fuck." All Refugio did was rock back and forth and breathe, quick and shallow, as though he was having an asthma attack.

The empty road in the moonlight looked post-apocalyptic. Shadows sliced across it like stripes on an army uniform. We never caught sight of Marlón.

Neither did anyone else, according to the soldier at the Villareal checkpoint. "What motorcycle?" he asked. He tried to order us off the road for violating curfew.

I really screamed then. Conspiracy, cover-up, bloody murder—which, unfortunately, was no exaggeration. I demanded that a search be launched. The soldier promised to get on his radio, but he probably only reported a redheaded maniac.

I drove off like a maniac. I'd found my tongue and couldn't shut up. If I had a theme, it was my mother's bogus mantra—*you create what you fear the most.* I must have repeated that line a dozen times. I badgered Refugio with the story of how my father dragged me into the yard one sunny morning when I was six years old. He'd wrapped his arms around me, covered my hands with his, and forced me to swing at hundreds of my brother's tricky overhand pitches while my mother and little sister looked on from the relative safety of the living room. I described in gory detail my father's rough red knuckles, the green garden hose winding through the grass like a snake, my mother's horrified expression behind the picture window. Once or twice a year my father would be seized by the urge to perform a fatherly duty. He'd smother one of us with an hour of attention. But his patience was razor-thin. "Hold still, goddammit—I'm doing this for you." That's what he'd hissed in my ear that morning. He'd treated me the way I treated Hércules, the way the United States treated Guatemala. "Hold still, goddammit—I'm doing this for you." My father loved baseball. I loathed baseball. You create what you fear the most.

I guess you had to be there. Although Refugio was there and he just kept rocking.

Do *you* follow my logic?

The important thing is that *I* followed it. From Villareal to Casa Schultz, my clarity was pure and absolute. All the contradictory truths, the ruthless, mercurial forces of the world, revealed themselves under the full moon. I saw the brutal flip side of creation.

And yet, when I lurched into Hoover's study, I wasn't ready. I wasn't ready to catch my fiancée and my friend *in flagrante delicto*.

I have a theory. I'm afraid it shows how dirty-minded I am, but I can't help it. Sometimes I suspect that Armando and Magdalena didn't stop at sweet talk on that couch. Sometimes I suspect that Armando wrote his whole manuscript in order to fool me about what went on between them. I hope I'm wrong. Armando never could keep a secret. But I'm resigned to my suspicions. Maybe I deserve them. A liar suspects lies. A cardsharp suspects marked cards. It's no big surprise what a fucker suspects.

XIII

GRIEF *(continued)*

"Where's your brother?" Spoon asked Magdalena, his voice as ominous as Aunt Martha's growl.

"What's wrong?" Magdalena said.

"Just quit your smooching for half a second and tell me where your brother is."

Magdalena had let go of my hand, but my legs still stretched across her lap. I couldn't move them quickly. She stared at Spoon with her chin raised high, as if the delicate curve of her neck constituted her best answer.

"Your brother murdered Hércules," Spoon said.

Magdalena's face seemed to lose its fine structure. Her whole body collapsed inward, like a building detonated from within. She covered her eyes with her fingertips and quietly trembled while Spoon stood at a distance and guzzled my beer.

"She needs you to hold her," I said to him. "I'm going to put on some shoes."

As I hobbled around the coffee table, Spoon looked at me for the first time.

"What happened to your nose?" he said.

"I think she's in bad shape," I said.

"Hércules is dead. I can't believe it."

When I hobbled back a few minutes later, Spoon was pacing at the far end of the room, jabbing his finger at a map. The drawers of Hoover's desk had been flung open. Magdalena sat rigid on the edge of the couch, eyes bloodshot, chest visibly rising and falling. Aunt Martha prowled between them.

"He sleeps in an annex next to the National Palace, but he could be anywhere," Spoon said, less to me than to the map.

"You'll never find him if he doesn't wish to be found," Magdalena said.

"I'll find him," Spoon said.

"Patricio, I'm terribly, terribly sorry about what happened to your friend, but you can't raise the dead."

"You coming?" Spoon asked me.

"Nothing you do will change the way it is in this country," Magdalena said. "Let the brutes have it. They have it already."

Spoon crumpled the map. "My life is so fucked up right now," he whispered.

Magdalena approached him cautiously, as if he was electrified. Aunt Martha kept between them, her haunches stiff with tension.

When Magdalena offered Spoon her hand, he swiped at it. Not hard—he didn't even touch her—but Aunt Martha lunged. Teeth snapped. Magdalena half pounced, half fell on the dog, crooked one arm around its neck, and slapped it firmly across the nose. She held the dog till it stretched out on the floor and covered its nose with its paws.

Spoon said nothing. A horn honked in the driveway. Spoon just dropped the map and trotted out.

Magdalena hugged her knees. She seemed determined to make herself as small as possible. I touched her shoulder, and she laid her wet cheek on my hand briefly, before we followed Spoon outside.

The Schultz family Mercedes couldn't pull up to the front door because Hércules' Peterbilt already occupied that spot. Spoon was climbing onto the running board when Refugio evidently released the clutch. The truck lurched forward and stalled. The Mercedes honked. Spoon brandished his middle finger. The far rear door of the Mercedes swung open and Hoover barreled out like a groggy bull.

"Did you order the murder of Hércules?" Spoon shouted.

"Pepito," Hoover called to the doorman. "Escort Mrs. Schultz into the house. My daughter also."

Spoon met Hoover in the narrow space between the Mercedes and the truck.

"Your son murdered Hércules tonight," Spoon said.

"My son?" Hoover said.

"The one with the Harley."

"He was identified?"

"I heard his motorcycle."

Hoover smoothed the lapels of his dinner jacket. Connie had already been ushered inside, but Magdalena lingered in the doorway with Pepito. Beto and I, like seconds at a duel, stationed ourselves a few steps from Hoover and Spoon.

"This is not the place to discuss such a grave accusation," Hoover said.

"You're right," Spoon said. "I'm going to the annex to have Marlón arrested."

"Out of the question," Hoover said.

"With all due respect, the decision is mine."

In the dim red glow of the taillights, Spoon crowded Hoover closer and closer, so that Hoover was forced to tilt his head back sharply in order to look him in the eye.

Hoover shrugged his massive shoulders. "Let's go then," he said.

"You're not coming," Spoon said.

"You would never find him without me," Hoover said.

"I know where the annex is."

"Yes, and you know where the White House is. And the Kremlin. Seriously, Patricio, who would be arrested? My son? The lieutenant? Spare yourself the humiliation."

"I'm sorry, but I don't want you to come along."

"With all due respect, the decision is mine."

Spoon reluctantly jerked his thumb at the back of the truck. "Hop in," he said.

"Please," Hoover said. "A little consideration for an old man who needs comfort." He indicated the open door of the Mercedes.

Spoon whistled for Refugio.

"Your friend should stay here," Hoover said. "Both your friends."

"Armando can stay—if he'd rather hang out with Magdalena."

"Grow up," I said.

Through the sepia-tinted windshield of the Mercedes, I watched Magdalena watch us from the doorway, her slim frame upright as ever, her face nearly blank but not quite. There was a quality in her guarded expression, the quality that gave her reserve so much emotional torque, which I hadn't been able to recognize up close but which from a distance revealed itself like the face of the moon. That quality was grief.

XIV

THE GREAT NO

For some people there's a day
when they have to come out with the great Yes
or the great No.
C. P. CAVAFY

"Things aren't always what they appear in situations like this," Hoover said.

"Situations like this?" Spoon said. "You mean murder?"

The quiet purr of the Mercedes was all we heard for a while. The midnight streets were practically deserted except for an occasional pair of soldiers. Sunk deep into plush leather, I massaged the back of my neck while Spoon cracked his knuckles and Refugio huddled over his rosary beads.

"Patricio," Hoover said. "I will use my influence to get us inside, but you must promise not to raise cain. It would put me in a very sensitive position. Understood?"

"I understand you."

"We have entirely too much vigilantism in our country already. Better to allow the system to do its work. Take advantage of the proper channels."

"Trust me," Spoon said.

Of course I didn't trust him. I put my hand over my heart and happened to feel the smooth, hard canister of mace. It inspired no confidence.

Across the plaza from the National Palace, the annex lurked in the shadows like the architectural equivalent of an unmarked car. The sullen guards stationed at its modest entrance examined Hoover's VIP card with none of the usual show of respect.

"It's very late," one of them said. "Perhaps in the morning."

The other one spit tobacco juice through a gap between his teeth.

"Mr. Schultz respectfully asserts his rights as an esteemed citizen of Guatemala," Spoon said.

I don't know what he would have done if Hoover had given up, but Hoover was not a man to tolerate a slight under any circumstances. "I am Hoover Carbajal García Schultz. This is a matter of urgent family business."

The tobacco-chewing soldier shambled up the stairs to a dialless telephone, spoke for a moment, spit half a dozen times, spoke again, and hung up.

"Come," he said. He deposited his chaw in a baby-food jar and herded us inside.

We followed him down a long corridor of bare walls and closed doors, silent and bright, with the antiseptic smell of an infirmary. A dozing soldier at a tiny desk roused himself to wave us down a virtually identical corridor, at the end of which sat a virtually identical soldier, this one busy arranging paper clips into an elaborate design. He directed us through the door behind him, which led to a commons room where five men sat in a cloud of cigarette smoke playing cards and drinking beer. Marlón was one of the men.

"We'll just finish this hand," he called over the heavy-metal music blaring from a tape deck on the floor.

"Where's your motorcycle?" Spoon demanded.

"*Momentito*," Marlón said. "My luck is running hot."

Spoon slapped his hands down on the card table. "Where's your motorcycle?" he said again.

"Patience, *cuñado*. Remember your breeding."

Spoon stepped back and lifted the card table high enough to topple all the beer bottles and send the money flying. One of the cardplayers pulled a revolver out of a holster looped around the back of his chair. Marlón just laughed.

"What a hot-blooded North American," he said.

Spoon kicked the tape deck as far as he could in flip-flops. It rolled under the bumper pool table, speakers up. The electric guitars continued to wail.

"Patricio, you promised," Hoover said. "Please, please excuse him. One of his Indians was found dead."

"He wasn't *found dead*. He was murdered by a man who escaped on a motorcycle. Where's your motorcycle, Marlón?"

Marlón rocked back his chair and put his feet up on the table. He seemed to enjoy the precarious position.

"First of all," Hoover said to Spoon, "you must show respect. In return Marlón will answer our questions. Have you been here all evening, my son?"

"Nowhere else, Papá."

"Could you prove it?"

Marlón simply shrugged his hands at the other men.

"You see?" Hoover said. "You were mistaken. Our answer lies elsewhere."

Spoon pointed at Marlón. "If you've been here all night, then your motorcycle should be cold. You won't object if we check it out?"

"Unfortunately, it's in the shop, *cuñado.*"

"And where's your gun?"

"Bend over and I'll conduct a thorough search," Marlón said, still rocking back and forth, grinning.

Hoover clamped a hand on Spoon's pointed finger and forced it down. "Behave, both of you," Hoover said. "We're civilized men."

Spoon whirled on Hoover. "Was it your idea? Did you tell him to do it?"

"Patricio, don't blame me because you couldn't keep your Indian out of the election. Don't blame my son. Your Indian, no doubt, had plenty of enemies of his own."

"Marlón was supposed to provide security for the election, remember?"

"I'm sure he had important business here."

"What? This card game?"

Hoover turned to Marlón. "Is there a more private place . . . ?"

"My colleagues will give us a few minutes. *Muchachos?*"

The man with the revolver glared at Spoon.

"Don't worry," Marlón said. "Come back in half an hour and I'll win the rest of your money." When the man still hesitated, Marlón added with a laugh, "If it gets too quiet in here, start shooting."

While the cardplayers swaggered out, Spoon paced, Refugio prayed, and Hoover enthroned himself opposite his son.

"Let's get this settled now," Hoover said. "We have the union of two great families to protect."

"I want Marlón to confess to the murder of Hércules Gavilán."

"Pull the plug on this *juevón.*"

"Patricio, be reasonable. Your accusation is based on nothing more than the sound of a motorcycle."

"I know he did it. And I won't leave until he confesses."

"Then you'll have to bunk with one of the other boys, because in my bed you're not welcome."

Spoon stopped pacing just behind Marlón. He crossed his arms like a man in a straitjacket. His breathing slowed. "I guess I'm being unreasonable," he said.

Marlón tipped back even further. He had no glimmer of what Spoon's sudden calm portended.

Spoon unbuttoned a shirtsleeve, deftly slipped out Hércules' knife, and held it to Marlón's throat.

"Don't move," Spoon said as blood spurted just above Marlón's Adam's apple.

Marlón's chair wobbled. His feet on the table squirmed. He could have reached back and grabbed Spoon's arms, but his throat would have been slit.

"Drop that knife this instant," Hoover said.

"First he tells me what I need to hear."

"Patricio, a confession extracted under these circumstances would be meaningless."

"No, it wouldn't," Spoon said.

The lower half of Marlón's neck ran bright red, a shiny, artificial red, the color of maraschino cherries. Marlón raised his hands, but not like a prisoner—more like a doctor before surgery. He tried to speak but couldn't because Spoon's hand covered most of his mouth. Spoon adjusted his grip.

"What if I killed him?" Marlón said. "What then?"

"Give me details. Verifiable details. What gun did you use? Where is it? Who ordered this?"

"I didn't do it," Marlón said. "I was just asking." His high-pitched whine sounded almost cocky. His pale blue eyes glittered with contempt.

"Put down the knife, Patricio," Hoover said. "Suppose that my son did kill your Indian, which is preposterous, but just for a moment suppose. He still deserves an impartial hearing the same as anyone else. You can't take the law into your own hands. Remember the rules of fair play, Patricio."

"That's not good enough," Spoon said.

"I assure you he was here all night. And if he wasn't here, he was acting under orders that cannot be revealed."

"Whose orders?"

"Don't throw away your life, Patricio—"

"He won't throw away shit," Marlón said. "And not because he's an angel, either. No, he's a rabbit-heart. An intellectual with a bow tie instead of balls. You sicken me, *cuñado*. That's what I confess. You sicken me."

As the crooked vein down the middle of Spoon's forehead throbbed and Marlón's black boots jiggled out of control, I saw a strong resemblance between these two boyish men, both determined to be cool.

Blood seeped onto Marlón's yellow shirt. I knew that warm, sticky feeling. I would have confessed by now, whether I'd committed a crime or not. But Marlón seemed almost indifferent to the spilling of his own blood. He had a taste for violence, an appetite, which Spoon lacked. Spoon was too attached to the pleasures of life to kill anyone. I doubted his capacity to slit Marlón's throat. I admit it. But I also wished him the courage to do the right thing for the right reason, out of strength instead of weakness.

The heavy-metal music clicked to a stop. Hoover's urgently drumming fingers filled the silence. Spoon forced Marlón's head back an inch further.

Marlón gurgled. "It's easy for the coward to cock the gun. It's difficult to pull the trigger."

Spoon drew the knife across Marlón's neck, lightly, like a violin bow, just above the Adam's apple. It was impossible to tell how deep the new cut went, but more blood flowed. Marlón's feet stiffened. "We have three problems, Papá," he said, his high, shaky voice striving for calm. "This skinny fool should lose his nerve in a minute. No need to worry there. The peasant is not much of a threat. He must be questioned, of course, about his role in the incident. But that one," he flicked his eyes at me, "the Indian from the United States—he acts suspicious."

"What do you think, Armando?" Spoon said.

My first instinct was to pretend I hadn't heard. I felt sure Spoon expected me to do the sensible thing, and I didn't want that burden. It occurred to me with the startling impact of the obvious that this was the pattern of our friendship: he led me to the edge and I dragged him back. I was always the one who exercised caution. I was always the one who said *no* to his *yes*. I shuffled closer to the table, but I would rather have stayed in the shadows like Refugio praying over his rosary beads.

"It's not worth it," I said. "You've got too much to lose."

Spoon compressed his blanched lips. His puffy face dripped big drops of sweat. "I've got nothing," he said. "Nothing but debts."

"Poor little *culero*," Marlón said.

"Shut up," Spoon said, his knife hand white at the knuckles.

Slowly, deliberately, I reached into my pocket and pulled out the mace. Spoon recognized it but didn't try to defend himself. I sprayed Marlón first to keep him from taking advantage of Spoon, and then I sprayed Spoon.

The mace acted no faster than I did. Marlón blinked, blinked, blinked, until his eyes shut tight. Spoon dropped the knife and turned away, sagging to his knees. Marlón clutched his neck, as if to meld the skin back together, and moaned high in his throat.

"I'm sorry," I said to Spoon, who cringed at my touch. His chest heaved. He vomited on my shoes.

I offered him a handkerchief, but he wouldn't accept it. He just slobbered out of control while Hoover whispered to Marlón. I cleaned my shoes with a playing card. Hoover discreetly slipped the knife into his dinner jacket and called in the soldiers.

"We've had a slight accident," he said. "Telephone Dr. Manfreddi at once."

Refugio found an unspilled beer and rinsed Spoon's mouth with it. He poured a little on his sleeve and wiped Spoon's face.

"See that the Indian receives transportation back to his village," Hoover said to the man with the revolver.

Refugio bowed. "I can get home on my own," he said softly.

"Nonsense," Hoover said. "These men will look after you."

Refugio kept his head down, but I heard the rattle of his rosary beads as his hands trembled.

"Mr. Schultz," I said. "Are you sure he'll be safe?"

Hoover glared at me in exasperation. Blood from the knife had begun to soak through his dinner jacket, forming a dark spot opposite his heart. I must have stared right at it because Hoover removed his jacket and scowled as if I'd accused him of a crime.

"I suppose there's room in the servants' quarters," he said.

Refugio's head bobbed in appreciation. "Many thanks," he said, lifting Spoon by the armpits.

Spoon's unsteady legs dangled like a marionette's. Refugio and I each took a side and half walked, half dragged Spoon out the door and down the first long corridor, his mouth wide open and his eyes pressed closed, oblivious how much of his weight rested on our shoulders.

X V

SOMETHING OR SOMEONE
HAD GONE AWAY

Between living and dreaming
Comes a third thing.

Guess what it is.
ANTONIO MACHADO

No one rousted me out of bed the next morning. I lingered under the covers and listened to the trees rustle in the wind. Branches slapped against the house. Wind chimes clanged. It was restless weather.

The sun shone through the small oval window above the desk, casting flickering shadows on the canister of mace. I didn't want to get up, but I couldn't forget that Hércules was dead and Spoon needed help. I goaded myself to the shower, which reminded me of Spoon because it ran very hot or very cold, so that I had to twirl the spigots constantly to keep the water a reasonable temperature. According to the bathroom's antique mirror, I looked better than I felt. The only signs of damage were a slight swelling of the nose and dull yellow rings under the eyes.

Downstairs, Magdalena's mother, Connie, was holding forth in the study, assigning the servants their wedding duties.

"The walls must also be mopped," she said as I slipped past.

I knocked once on Spoon's door out of custom, the way you knock when you expect a room to be empty. I was hoping to find a note telling me where to meet him, at the police station or the American Embassy, but there he lay, buried under frilly covers, big feet protruding over the end of the high poster bed. Magdalena lay next to him on top of the covers. Her black slippers seemed meant to indicate that she was on the bed as opposed to in it.

"Thank you," she whispered.

"For what?" I said.

"You saved him," she said. "He'll be all right now."

She dismissed me with a tired smile that I couldn't return. The title of the book cracked open on her lap was *A Traveler's Guide to Connecticut.*

There must have been times when Spoon slept later than I did, a dreadful hangover or a severe case of the flu, but all I could remember was the usual pattern: Spoon bounding out of bed, taking the first shower, cranking up the stereo, and if I still hadn't budged, he'd whistle in my ear or tickle my feet. And yet now, on this crucial day, I was up and he wasn't.

Connie spotted me from the study and called my name. "Armando, have you been measured? Are you familiar with your sizes offhand? There's a tape measure here somewhere. Where's Patricio? My husband spoke to Patricio's parents very early this morning and they're flying in tonight. They may be able to join us at the rehearsal dinner if their flight is on time. Isn't that marvelous? You'll look impressive in a tuxedo. You have the necessary girth. But this tape measure. Why do things cease to exist just when you need them? Cielita, fix Armando bread and coffee."

"Excuse me," I said. "Do you know where Refugio is?"

"Who?"

"Patricio's friend. He stayed here last night. In the servants' quarters."

"I'm afraid I wouldn't have any idea. You might ask Cielita."

"Is don Hoover at home?"

"I ran him off hours ago. The *jefe* and his *mayordomo* always have plenty of manly business to attend to, thank God. Which reminds me—why don't you take Patricio for a manicure or a haircut? He's a lovely boy, but that haircut is a horror. Just make sure you're back here by six o'clock. And be sure to tell Patricio that his parents are on the way. Is the wife extremely pretty?"

Outside, the whistling wind stirred up funnel-shaped spouts of gravel and dust, especially right in front of the house where Hércules' truck had been parked, almost as if the absence of the truck agitated the air as much as it agitated me.

"*Se fué*," the doorman Pepito said, employing to full advantage the ambiguity of Spanish. Something or someone had gone away.

"Where?" I asked.

"Who knows?" Pepito said, arching his bushy eyebrows.

I followed the stone path to the back of the house. Wet white tablecloths flapped on a rope stretched between posts. There was a truck of sorts, but it was only a florist's van pulled up to the kitchen. I checked out the servants' quarters, which consisted of a men's wing and a women's wing separated by a laundry room, where a pair of large washing machines rattled and shook as if possessed by a force more demonic than the spin cycle.

I felt like a spy wandering among the bunk beds, a bumbling spy patting the bare straw mattresses, jiggling the locks on the footlockers. What was I doing here? It occurred to me, as the wind whipped the trees, that the worst days of my childhood, the worst *average* days, had been windy like this. My muscles would weaken, my brain would go numb, so that I couldn't do anything and I couldn't do nothing. I'd breathe on the window, count each tick of the clock, shrink from the terrible shaking of the trees. The wind seemed to insist that I had no place in the world. I was incidental, like dust. When Pepito suddenly appeared at my shoulder, I shuddered.

"Your breakfast has been served in the dining room," he said. The wind tousled his bristly white hair so that the spotted dome of his skull shone through. I saw him as a figure in a dream I might wake up from at any second to discover Hércules alive, Refugio safe, Spoon and Magdalena happy and in love. That was the kind of solution I craved: miraculous, complete. Otherwise, I needed someone to tell me what to do. I needed Spoon.

"After you," Pepito said.

"Wait," I said. "Did Patricio's friend sleep here last night?"

"Yes, sir," Pepito said. He tried to usher me out, but I wouldn't budge.

"Where is Patricio's friend now?"

Pepito shrugged.

"When you went out front this morning, was the red truck still there?"

Pepito nodded once, grudgingly.

"And were you at the front door when the truck was driven away?"

He pushed his disheveled hair more or less into place. "I believe so. I wasn't paying much attention."

"Who drove, please?"

"Let me think," Pepito said. "I believe the Indian and the *mayordomo* were in the truck. Maybe, yes, he was going to show him the road back to the country, back to his home. Yes, that was it." Pepito wiped his mouth with the palm of his hand.

"And don Hoover?"

"The *jefe* took the Mercedes."

"He drove?"

"He often drives. Now please come eat your breakfast or the señora will have words with me."

"I'm not hungry," I said.

Pepito wiped his mouth again, as if to get rid of a bad taste.

Magdalena's strained voice carried to the hallway. I didn't eavesdrop, but I heard what she was saying as I knocked:

"I just want clarity, darling."

I knocked again. "It's Armando," I said.

"Oh, good," she said, struggling to sound sweet. "Maybe you can help this wretched man."

She stood at the window, gazing out. I wondered if the wind affected her as it affected me.

Spoon lay in the middle of the sagging bed, wrapped in white covers like a mummy.

"How are you?" I said.

He opened his mouth but didn't speak.

"Patricio is not feeling well," Magdalena said.

"Are you sick?" I asked him.

"What do you care?" he said.

"We have a lot to do."

"Like what?"

"I'm not exactly sure of the appropriate steps. If Marlón killed Hércules—"

Spoon's hand fluttered out from under the covers and slapped the bed in disgust.

"I'm worried about Refugio, too," I said. "Evidently, he's driving the truck back to Santa Catalina."

"He can't drive worth a damn," Spoon said. "He must have really wanted to get home."

"Let's roll," I said. "You might not know it in here, but the wedding machine is gearing up out there. You should probably tell Connie if . . ."

"If what?" Spoon said.

Magdalena turned from the window. "The wedding goes forward as planned."

"Hell, they can conduct the ceremony right here," Spoon said. "I'm not leaving this bed until I have a reason."

"Your parents are coming," I said.

Spoon didn't seem to stir, but the bed squeaked.

"Hoover called them this morning," I said.

"They're not taking any chances, boy. Send in the marines. Bring up the heavy artillery."

Magdalena pressed her trembling fingertips together. "He needs rest," she said with a pointed glance toward the door.

"That mace is a bitch," Spoon said.

"You'll feel a lot better after a shower," I said.

Magdalena hooked her arm around mine. "Let him sleep," she said. "Please."

"There are things we have to do," I said.

"*Wait un-til af-ter the wed-ding,*" she said, enunciating so clearly that I heard a trace of fear between each syllable.

"I'm sorry," I said. I took her hands and kissed them.

"How about a little respect for the groom?" Spoon said.

"Please, Patricio, don't act like a brute," Magdalena said. "I put my faith in you. Remember that, at least, if you must seek trouble. We can be very, very happy. We just have to survive this difficult time."

"Too bad Hércules couldn't survive it," Spoon said.

Magdalena bumped the door frame on her way out.

"What's keeping *you*?" Spoon asked me.

I yanked off his covers and threw them onto the floor. He just crossed his legs in one of his favorite contortionist positions. "You stupid jerk," he said.

"There must be someone in authority who can help us."

"I don't trust you," he said, oozing off the bed, arms and head first. "I feel like dead skin," he moaned from the floor. "I wish I could shed this life and start over."

"It's the wind," I said. "It must be the wind."

XVI

QUIXOTE WITH A K

And I have seen the dust from the walls of institutions
Finer than flour, alive, more dangerous than silica,
Sift, almost invisible, through long afternoons of tedium,
Dropping a fine film on nails and delicate eyebrows,
Glazing the pale hair, the duplicate gray standard faces.
THEODORE ROETHKE

The National Police Headquarters depended on guilt the way a
hospital depends on sickness or a church depends on despair.
Tramping its formidable hallways, I imagined being slapped in
handcuffs and locked in a cell, unable to plead my innocence.
The green walls absorbed what little light penetrated the high
vaulted windows. The gray stone floors inspired dread.

When I asked the secretary in the stuffy anteroom of the
Office of the Chief of Detectives if this was the proper place to
report a murder, she said, "Homicide. Very good."

The overhead fan squeaked above us. She lit a brown cigarette and ordered us to sit.

"Show her your VIP card," I said to Spoon.

"Why bother?" he said.

He seemed determined to make me do the work, so I presented the card myself. The secretary reluctantly put down her
cigarette smeared with violet lipstick and held the card up to
the fluorescent light.

"Foreigners?" she said.

"North Americans," I said.

"Whatever," she said. "You must sit."

We sat long enough for me to notice that the secretary's pan-
cake makeup covered an extraordinary amount of facial hair,
that nothing moved behind the opaque yellow panel in the
Chief of Detectives' door, that the fan squeaked on every fourth
beat, and that Spoon's sighs grew deeper and deeper.

"You think it's a coincidence?" I asked him. "What we both
went through? I mean, I was basically kidnapped. People de-

bated whether to kill me. I licked a pair of boots to save my life. And you—murder. How do you figure it? Both of us at the same time. *Bad things happen in threes* is what my mother always says. Which used to seem like the most ignorant superstition, but now I wonder if certain events are charged with a kind of magnetism. Do you believe in the magnetism of charged events? Because in my experience, disaster attracts disaster, I'm absolutely sure."

Spoon just cracked his neck.

"When will the Chief of Detectives be finished in there?" I snapped at the secretary.

"Detective Soto isn't in there," the secretary said. "He's at lunch."

Spoon laughed, a short, mirthless explosion of breath, full of derision, as if he alone comprehended the full absurdity of the world.

A telephone across the hall rang and rang. I clenched my hands into fists and slowly unclenched them.

Detective Soto must have had cake for lunch—he kept picking crumbs off his rumpled tweed jacket.

"How m-may I h-help you?" he asked with a dignified stutter.

Spoon gazed at the ceiling to let me know he wouldn't answer.

"A friend of ours was shot and killed last night," I said.

"In which zone?" Detective Soto said.

"Zone?" I said.

"The city is divided into z-z-zones," Detective Soto said.

"It didn't happen here in the city," I said. "It happened at a coffee *finca*."

"And wh-wh-where is this *f-finca*?" Detective Soto asked.

I elbowed Spoon. "The *boca costa*," he said. "Southeast of Monte Alto."

"Unfortunately, that's outside my juris-d-diction," Detective Soto said. His delighted smile revealed a pair of shiny gold molars.

"Then who the hell do we have to talk to?" I said.

Spoon laughed as he had before, the same mean-spirited bark of a laugh.

"Excuse me, Detective," I said.

"There's Sergeant G-G-Garralaga on the f-fourth floor. You're North Americans, no? Why don't you try the Legal Affairs Bureau at the N-N-National Palace? Humberto Gomez is on top of everything."

"Are you sure?" I said.

"I'll have my secretary phone ahead."

"Thank you for your kind efforts," Spoon said.

"At your service," Detective Soto said. He positively beamed, as if nothing pleased him more than showing off his gold teeth.

Spoon maintained a hostile silence as we weaved our way toward the National Palace, alternately swept along and stymied by the swarms of shoppers on Sixth Avenue.

"Do the police here seem like amateurs to you?" I asked him. "Like law enforcement is a hobby?"

He grunted.

"I never thought I'd wax nostalgic about the Mission Station, but I miss those vending machines. I even miss Conway Twitty."

Despite Sixth Avenue's profusion of gaudy billboards, flapping banners, and elaborate window displays, I kept thinking of my ordeal, remembering details I wanted to tell Spoon. When the commandante had rummaged through my belongings, I'd been embarrassed almost to the point of humiliation by the number of personal hygiene products: soap, shampoo, toothpaste, deodorant, shaving cream, aftershave, skin lotion, nail clippers, Q-tips, dental floss. Real humiliation, though, was crying uncontrollably while the jittery private had jabbed me from behind with his rifle. Yet I'd reached a point where the crying felt good. I'd actually laughed inside at the idea that I was protecting myself not with cleverness or strength but with hysterical sobbing. Spoon had no interest in hearing these things.

The sky appeared above the Parque Central, brown and thick as gravy. A chunk of grit blew into my eye.

"I need a drink," Spoon said. "In the worst way."

The National Palace was so opulent that even the Legal Affairs Bureau had a breathtaking painting of a Mayan temple hanging behind the secretary's desk. A crystal chandelier filled the anteroom with a festive saffron light. The secretary himself, a baby-faced cream puff with pallid cheeks and a thin black mustache, seemed far less festive. He unctuously demanded our passports.

"I'm sorry," I said. "My passport was stolen."

"Has the theft been reported?"

"No. Well, yes. The army officer who found me wrote a report, I believe."

"Your copy, please?"

"I don't have it with me."

"Bring it in tomorrow. Now, where precisely did this theft occur?"

"Near a town called Maluatla. The department of El Quiche."

"I'm afraid—" the secretary began, but Spoon interrupted.

"Our appointment is with Humberto Gomez," he said.

"Lieutenant Gomez has no appointments today," the secretary said. "Lieutenant Gomez is on vacation."

"Jesus Christ," I said.

"Don't tell me you're still surprised," Spoon said. He wearily slapped his VIP card on the mahogany desk.

"This is not a passport," the secretary said.

"It's the architecture," Spoon explained to me in English. "The architecture brings out the fascist in everybody. You know, the president who built this dump worshipped Mussolini. He wore leather riding outfits just like *Il Duce,* even though horses scared the crap out of him. For awhile he sported the same kind of mustache as this little twerp. Listen, *amigo,*" Spoon switched back to Spanish, "we wish to report a murder. Political assassination. Isn't there anyone around here with ears?"

"Once it has been ascertained that your papers are in order, I will gladly assist you," the secretary said. "Your passports, please."

"Did Detective Soto call you a little while ago?" I said.

"Who?" the secretary said.

Spoon plucked a fountain pen from a gold penholder and shoved it into the secretary's hand. "A man named Hércules Prieta Gavilán was shot and killed with an automatic weapon at the *finca* La Esperanza southeast of Monte Alto. The murderer was Marlón de Montenegro Schultz, who works just down the street on the first floor of the annex. Should I repeat?"

"Are you a relative of the deceased?"

Spoon clapped his hands less than an inch from the secretary's upturned nose. The secretary merely blinked. I grabbed Spoon by the shoulder and pulled him away from the desk. He was easier to move than I expected. I felt the hard knob of his collarbone, the scant flesh protecting it. Spoon had never seemed frail before.

"It's nice to see the old Spoon," I said. "But maybe the old Spoon should cool it a little."

"The old Spoon is dead."

"There are procedures which must be followed in any official inquiry," the secretary said.

"Forget it," Spoon said. "But let me warn you, comrade, that we are field inspectors from the Office of Bureaucratic Competence. An evaluation of your performance this afternoon will be filed with all appropriate agencies."

"If there really has been a murder," the secretary said, "you must report to the head of police in the department where it occurred."

"I need a drink," Spoon said.

"Your names, please?" the secretary said.

"Quixote," I said. "With a *K.*"

XVII

ALBONDIGAS

How good to know
Glasses are for drinking;
How troubling to wonder
Why we thirst.

ANTONIO MACHADO

We adjourned to Albóndigas, Spoon's favorite bar in Guatemala, a cool dark basement dive tucked below a pool hall. Spoon installed us on swivel stools at the massive marble-topped bar. A cloudy mirror reflected our troubled faces. Propped against the old-fashioned cash register was a faded placard with the single word *ALBONDIGAS*—which means *meatballs*—stenciled in red block letters.

"Yo, Larry," Spoon said in English to the bartender, a white-haired black man busy slicing limes. "Two of your primo margaritas, if you please."

"Just a glass of bottled water for me," I said.

"He'll have a margarita," Spoon said.

"I'm not drinking on this empty stomach," I said. "And you shouldn't either."

"You're embarrassing me in front of Larry," Spoon said. "How about I eat if you drink?"

"If it makes you happy, I'll have a beer and the meatballs."

"Excuse us," Spoon said to Larry, who just went on slicing limes in devout silence while I followed Spoon to the privacy of a booth. "Don't order the meatballs," Spoon whispered with disconcerting vehemence. "They taste like turpentine."

I couldn't help laughing. Spoon gaped at me as if I'd slapped him and then he burst out laughing too. We stood right next to each other and laughed ourselves to tears.

Over bland black beans and mediocre margaritas, I advised Spoon to postpone the wedding.

"Ah," he said. "A glimpse of motive. You want Magdalena for yourself, don't you?"

"The wedding just seems wrong to me," I said.

"And making out on the couch seems right?"

"The wedding seems wrong," I said again. "It's like an endorsement of the murder. Why not postpone the wedding until there's been some kind of investigation, or elope without all the family trappings?"

Spoon swiveled around on his stool and grabbed my knees. "Why'd you mug me last night?" he said.

"I'm sorry if you think I let you down," I said.

"*Let me down?*" he said. "You *let me down* when you abandoned your marriage. This was *betrayal*. Does the name Benedict Arnold ring a bell? How about Judas?"

"We should probably call Magdalena," I said. "The rehearsal dinner . . ."

"What do you care? You want me to blow off the whole shebang."

"No," I said. "I want you and Magdalena to talk things over. Reach a mutual decision."

"She'd flip out," Spoon said.

He asked Larry for the telephone, dialed, and handed the receiver to me. Magdalena answered. I sucked in my gut.

"This is Armando," I said.

"Where are you? Is everything all right?"

Her voice was shot with worry. She drew a shallow breath, and just like that the truth changed. I couldn't tell her the same truth I'd told Spoon.

"Patricio's not feeling well. We may have to miss the rehearsal dinner."

"Where are you?" she said. "I want to be with *you*."

For a second I almost believed she meant *me*, not *us*, and I instinctively covered the mouthpiece. My heart pounded against my ribs. Spoon chewed an ice cube. I placed the phone to his ear.

"Hey, babe," he said.

"We're just cooling out at Albóndigas," he said.

"Just beer," he said. "Honest."

"I don't know," he said. "Armando thinks maybe we should postpone the wedding."

He handed the phone back to me. Magdalena had hung up.

"Picture the Starship Enterprise," Spoon said as he and I settled into a slick red vinyl booth. "Picture the Starship Enterprise after a devastating battle with the Klingons. Warp drive destroyed. Shields inoperative. Impulse power only. That's how I feel. Like I'm running on impulse."

It infuriated me that Spoon was only thinking of himself, that he was blathering about a TV show. "It's tough when your life stops being perfect," I said.

"My life stopped being perfect when I was eight years old."

"This is different," I said angrily. "You're an adult now. You're responsible."

"I don't *grok,*" Spoon said.

"People expect perfection. Maybe they don't admit it to themselves, but they go along for years believing life will get better and better, and then one day something happens and they realize what a fantasy their fantasy is. Suddenly, life is in charge, not you."

"That's very comforting, of course," Spoon said. "Thank you so much."

"I'm not trying to be comforting," I said. "I'm trying to explain a mistake I've lived through. I understand the urge to quit. Why play if you can't win? But what I'm starting to figure out is that you have to accept your weakness along with your strength."

"How Zen," Spoon said.

He glanced up as the door swung open. A group of office workers came jostling down the stairs. One of them plugged in the jukebox and punched up an old soul tune. The bartender lit the candles at the occupied tables.

"My mother used to warn us about pneumonia," Spoon said. "*Once you catch it once, you're more susceptible forever.* Last night when I found Hércules, I remembered finding my sister. I had the same weird sensation of susceptibility. A force worse than any virus had invaded my system, and it would never leave." He glared at me. "Perfection is not my hang-up. It must be yours."

The sight of Magdalena threw Spoon into gear. He switched my Coke with his margarita and stashed the empty glasses under the table.

"Don't tattle," he said, swaying to his feet. He flung his arms out for balance like a tipsy tightrope walker.

Everyone in the bar must have watched Magdalena stride down the stairs behind Aunt Martha. Not only was she young and beautiful—not only was she stunningly decked out in a black silk evening gown, pearls, and high heels—not only was she holding a German shepherd under a tight leash—but she had the brilliant intensity of a person in crisis. When Spoon tried to kiss her, she stopped him with sheer body language.

"Thank you for being here," she said.

"Sorry we screwed up the dinner," Spoon said. He and I both scooted over, but she preferred to stand.

"The dinner is fine. Your parents will join my parents and a few family friends at Escobar's Restaurant."

"Please sit down," Spoon said.

"I need to get things settled. Forgive my directness. Do you wish to marry me or not?"

Spoon didn't hesitate. "Marry you, *yes*. But the wedding is a problem. Do you believe your brother killed Hércules?"

"It's not impossible," Magdalena said.

"Do you believe your father told him to?"

"Marlón rarely heeds my father. Still . . . No, I don't believe he'd ruin my wedding."

"Armando thinks—and, well, I agree—this big extravaganza right after the murder sort of condones it somehow. It dishonors Hércules. Does that make sense to you?"

"What do you suggest as an alternative?"

"We could elope."

"Would you do that?"

"Yes."

"To leave Guatemala married to you would please me very much."

"Even without a monster wedding?"

"The purpose of the wedding is to satisfy my parents. Naturally, I'd rather have their blessing. It would . . . facilitate things." Magdalena tentatively perched on the edge of the booth. "It never occurred to me that you would defy my father."

"Me?" Spoon said. "Defy? Your father? Sure, I'll defy him. Our problems are solved."

He leaned over to hug Magdalena. She twisted toward him from the waist up. It was an awkward embrace.

"Patrick, I can't face my parents alone. Come with me to Escobar's."

"Let's celebrate first. Larry, margaritas all around."

"Seriously, Patricio, there are practical considerations. The wedding is *tomorrow.* Guests have been invited. We should try to minimize the inconvenience."

"How's this for a plan? We celebrate a little, then check into the Sheraton. Separate rooms. Propriety. Early in the morning, when folks are most reasonable, we call Casa Schultz. Maybe, if we're lucky, we can leave a message with Pepito."

Magdalena looked skeptical, but I was the one Spoon chose to confront.

"What's wrong, Armando? Not noble enough for you? You think we should go to Escobar's and lecture our elders on respect for the dead? Well, I can't stomach it. I'm a rabbit-heart, remember? I accept my weakness along with my strength."

The only response I could manage was a shrug.

Spoon shifted his attention to Magdalena. "Will you dance with me?" he said.

No one else was dancing. There was no designated dance floor and Magdalena certainly hadn't signaled any eagerness to dance. She rose with such solemn purpose that I expected her to storm out, but she reached back for Spoon and helped him up.

They held each other at a slight distance, barely moving to the bittersweet horns. A guitar sustained a clear major chord and Otis Redding implored whoever might be listening to try a little tenderness.

Spoon and Magdalena rocked back and forth, slowly turning in a tight circle. I accidentally caught Magdalena's eye and she quickly looked away while the hollow *tock* of drumstick against drumstick marked time at its most basic.

When the tempo quickened, almost as if Otis Redding had begun to convince himself that there was reason to hope, Spoon stepped back from Magdalena and then stepped in close. They did a serious slow-motion jitterbug that accelerated along with the music. Magdalena's bare shoulders shimmered in the candlelight. She no longer appeared to be conducting official business. She and Spoon joined hands like two kids playing ring-around-the-rosy and spun in front of the table faster and faster until Otis Redding's gritty voice reached a crescendo and they hugged, both of them squeezing just as hard, or so it seemed from where I sat, tearing my napkin into strips, wanting to believe but not believing that everything would be fine.

When I received my acceptance to law school, my wife and I drank a whole magnum of champagne. We were happy—I'm sure we were happy—but there was a tiny sliver of apprehension, a dread of the inevitable catch, as if now that our wish had been granted there had to be a loophole we'd overlooked, a voracious loophole that could only grow larger and larger until it consumed our wish and devoured us in the process.

Spoon made a valiant effort to distract Magdalena and me from the loophole. Tossing down double-strength margaritas, he recounted long stories about people in the Berkeley anthropology department. Magdalena listened politely, but she didn't touch her wine. She seemed too tense to swallow.

Spoon drank till he passed out. First he lay his head down on the table. Then he lay his head in Magdalena's lap and nestled into the curve of the booth. While he snored over a bluesy ballad, she tapped her fingernails against the stem of her wineglass. She hadn't said a word to me. I tried to ignore her graceful hands, the fragrance of her perfume, the provocative rustle of silk when she crossed her legs, but obviously I failed.

"I hope you don't think I'm against the marriage," I said. "I wish you and Patrick all the happiness in the world."

"All the happiness in the world," she repeated with almost no inflection, her eyes focused on the wineglass.

"You deserve it," I said.

"You don't know what I deserve," she said. "Shall we go?"

"Casa Schultz or the Sheraton?" I said.

She finally looked at me. Her expression softened a little. She began to drink her wine. "I have this friend," she said. "The friend I went to California with. The friend with the Volkswagen van. Technically, he's my cousin, but we're very distant."

I nodded as if I understood.

"His family was never as affluent as ours, but they sent him to the most expensive schools. *My* schools. He resented the sacrifice. In some ways Rogelio was very much like Patrick—rebellious, undisciplined, too smart for his own good.

"He played guitar beautifully. Classical, jazz, blues. He played with everybody. One of his musician friends worked for Coca-Cola. Rogelio played with him during a strike, to entertain the people walking the picket line. A car bomb went off and Rogelio was paralyzed. Even his face." Magdalena imitated her cousin's blank expression. The imitation was almost cruel. "For months he couldn't say a word. The hospital bills were astronomical. My father paid most of them. And I was very, very grateful." She looked away as if she'd finished the story.

"What about Rogelio?" I said.

"He lives at home now. But the bills are still outrageous. Far beyond what his family can afford. He wants a special computer you operate with a kind of wand in your mouth. His *mind* is active. He's not broken inside. It's just the wiring between the inside and the outside.

"I don't see him much anymore. I ran out of caring." She drank the last of her wine. "All gone," she said. She turned the wineglass over and shook out the last few drops.

"Everybody falls short," I said.

"When did you fall short?"

"Oh, God, my whole life."

"That's no answer."

Spoon raised his heavy head over the edge of the table, flashed a vacant grin, and flopped back down.

"My mother claims it's not *who* you meet but *when*," Magdalena said. "Patrick and I are drawn together by something I don't understand. Cold passion, if there is such a thing." She checked her watch. "I'm afraid to make a decision."

"So is he," I said.

"Casa Schultz or the Sheraton? You put it so well."

"You think your father might cut Rogelio off?"

She tilted her head to the side, as if I'd asked an indelicate question. I contemplated the prominent contours of her cheekbones, the faint worry lines etched in her soft young skin. I told her a story I'd never told anyone.

"Years ago, when I was trying to become a lawyer, I had to interview this woman whose four-year-old son had leukemia. The woman and her son lived in a tract house a block from our client's chemical plant. A full-fledged attorney came along to watch me show my stuff. I asked the woman how many packs a day she smoked, what brand of birth control pills she used, the circumstances of her marijuana bust. A private detective had already dug up the dirt on her. I'd written the questions. The whole point was to weaken her case against the chemical plant, but she treated my colleague and I like friends, and her little boy kept running up to us.

"He had almost no hair. It was a side effect of the leukemia treatment. Another side effect was something called heel cord shortening, which contracts the calf muscle and pulls up the heel so you can only walk on your toes. You need huge shoes to support your feet. The little boy wore these ugly, clunky shoes, but he kept clomping up to us and hugging our knees.

"It didn't seem to bother my colleague, but I wondered why I was there. I'd felt so clever writing those questions."

Magdalena blinked at me, as if she sensed my panic. The whole purpose of telling the story was to offer consolation, but the longer I went on, the more elusive consolation became.

"All I'm saying is that everybody falls short once in a while."

"What bullshit!" Spoon said, propping himself up on his elbows. "You dumped your wife, man. For a bald kid? My ass."

"Don't be a jerk," I said.

Magdalena patted my hand before she helped Spoon sit up. "Patrick, are you all right?"

He sang along in falsetto to the song on the jukebox.

"We should leave," Magdalena said.

He kissed her neck—a loud, wet smack. She enticingly backed out of the booth and he crawled after her, flopping onto the floor. Aunt Martha started to lick his face. Magdalena waited a deliberate second or two before she pulled the dog off him.

"Albóndigas!" he said. "Best bar in Guatemala. Just don't eat the meatballs."

"We need to figure out where to go," I said.

"I'm at your disposal," he said.

Magdalena winced.

"The Sheraton or Casa Schultz?" I said.

Spoon, despite being flat on his back, managed to shrug. "Let the dog decide," he said.

Magdalena jerked Aunt Martha by the leash and went to the bar to settle the bill. I hauled Spoon to his feet. He wrapped me in a bear hug.

"You dance divinely," he said, so I danced him toward the stairs. His breath reeked of tequila. "I don't believe we've been properly introduced," he said.

I caught a glimpse of our reflection in the cloudy mirror above the bar, him so loose and gangly, me so unalterably tense, as if my thick body were bound by ropes and wires, each tightened to a different stress.

"Remember the baker who drowned?" he said. "The little pile of stones on the shore of the lake? I was lucky enough to be invited to the funeral. They burned candles in every corner of the house. They spread flowers all around the coffin. The only time they ever pick flowers is for the dead. Interesting, no? They buried him with his hat, his apron, and his rolling pin. No kidding. His rolling pin. They'll have to bury Hércules with his truck."

Spoon tried to laugh, but it sounded like a karate grunt. Hércules was the loophole, I realized as Magdalena and I gingerly maneuvered Spoon up the stairs, through the empty pool hall checkered with blue shadows, and out to the Buick. "You take the high road and I'll take the low road," Spoon sang as we loaded him into the backseat.

"Where are we going?" I asked Magdalena.

"There's dog food at home," she said. "Aunt Martha is hungry."

XVIII

FATHERLY ADVICE

The thrill is gone.
The thrill is gone away.
B. B. KING

A funny thing happened on the way to the altar. On the way *from* the altar? Where the fuck was I headed? It's idle speculation. A moot point. Which is why I prefer not to think about my wedding day. I come to bury the past, not to praise it.

But seriously, folks. This is my last gap to fill in. My last gasp. Not that I enjoy stealing Armando's thunder.

Now there's an interesting phrase—*steal thunder*—from the Paiute legend of the coyote and the owl. Or was it the crow and the moody rain cloud?

I beg your pardon. My mind is wandering. Not to mention my tailbone aches and my scalp itches. But we're getting near the end. I smell the ocean. Fingers, don't fail me now.

Have you ever had a dream where you find yourself in a strange house, in a strange bedroom, and you can't remember how you got there? You lie naked under a thick comforter; you're dazed, disoriented, afraid to move; and all of a sudden you realize your father is with you?

It happened to me, in what Armando has the nerve to call *real life,* although it seemed more like one of his fever dreams.

My father was tapping on my already open door. He tapped with the head of his cane from the Philippines, his garish, hand-painted, eagle-headed cane. I remembered that cane from my childhood. I'd used it as a sword, a horse, a magic wand. The ugly ebony eagle painted red, white, and blue had always fascinated me, lurking among the dull umbrellas in every house we'd ever occupied. My father tapped lightly but persistently, until I covered my ears. I felt like a baby, naked and defenseless.

What was I afraid of? Birds, as Armando would have said,

chirped outside my window. Sunlight angled through the slats in the wicker blinds. The room wasn't even hot yet, although the early morning freshness wouldn't last much longer.

My father wheeled a glass-topped breakfast cart right up to the bed. He sat down near my feet where I could watch him. He looked dapper and pathetic at the same time. His sharp linen suit didn't fit quite right, too big in the shoulders, too small in the paunch, and the pants hiked up over his thin brown socks to expose the brittle, translucent shins of an old man. He cracked two eggs into a glass, shook in four squirts of Worcestershire sauce and three delicate drops of Tabasco, then stirred with the long end of a spoon. It was a shock to be reminded where my hangover cure came from.

My father winked as he stirred. He was operating in his good-buddy mode, turning on his cutesy charm. He handed me the glass and held his nose. I drank with true gratitude, and told him so. But he ruined the moment as soon as he spoke.

"At times like these, a family has to stick together," he said.

"Aren't you quick with a cliché," I said.

"There's a lot of truth in the old sayings." He planted both hands on the eagle-headed cane locked between his knees and faced away from me, toward the closed door, so that I saw him in profile, not only the strong line of his nose and chin but also the forlorn, question-mark curve of his spine. "How are you, son?" he said to the door.

"I'm fine. How are you?"

"Old and dying. But there's a little spark left." He waited for me to say something and then went on. He didn't need much help to hold a conversation. "Those long plane flights are a killer at my age. There's no *air* on those planes. By the way, thanks for letting us old farts get together on our own last night."

"Hmm," I said.

"I was sorry to hear about your Indian friend," he said.

"Yeah, people don't like to hear that stuff."

"You know what I mean. I'm sorry it happened."

"I'm sorry too. I'm sorry Magdalena's brother is a killer."

"It may not have been him," my father said.

"It may not have been Sirhan Sirhan."

My father made a production of taking a deep breath. "I think we ought to keep out of this one."

"You keep out. I'm already in."

"Frankly, son, you may be in over your head. I have some experience with lost causes. Don't forget I caught flack on the Bay of Pigs. There are some battles a man can't win."

"You got to know when to fold 'em," I said. I was quoting one of the century's worst songs, but my father completely missed my sarcasm.

"Now you're talking," he said. "We're both realists. We both know what's what. The system, imperfect as it is, is the best way to deal with a mess like this."

I kicked my father. I sort of kicked him. I stayed under the covers, but I slid my foot beneath his butt and lifted. "Pay attention," I said. "I plan to nail Marlón's ass."

My father looked at me. He nodded his head in a show of great understanding and compassion. "You could try," he said. "You could spend a lot of time and energy. But what would it get you?"

"I can't just drop it," I said.

My father shrugged, as if he might be willing to accept a standoff for now. "I only want what's best for you," he said.

"Cliché," I said.

"Sue me," he said. He smiled, a slightly self-deprecating smile, his most sympathetic pose. "I want to ask you a favor," he said. "Are you in love with Magdalena?"

"What's the favor?" I said.

He shifted the cane between his knees like a throttle. "Please. Do you want to marry her?"

I sat up straighter in the sagging bed. "Yeah."

My father built a little silence around my answer. "I want you, as a favor to me, your father, to marry Magdalena in the church this afternoon."

"What do you care where I marry her? I mean—no offense, Dad—but what's your angle?"

"Why aggravate the situation? If you're going to marry her anyway, why not mend a few fences? The Latin people put a lot of stock in these big occasions. A lot of face is involved."

"Who gives a fuck about face?"

"Hoover does." My father wiped his eyes. His eyes watered when he got excited. He found his nitroglycerin and popped a pill under his tongue. He was trying, obviously, not to lose his temper. "To tell you the truth, this is Hoover's idea. *He* asked *me* a favor. I really can't explain why he's so fixated on this wedding. I do know that Magdalena humiliated him once in the past at some major social function. I gather she called him a back-stabbing bastard in front of half the bigwigs in Guatemala. And yet he still worships her. They have a complicated relationship." My father thumped the cane against the floor like a carnival horse doing arithmetic.

I wished I had clothes on. "Well, you've done your bit for Hoover. You must be more loyal than I am. Because to me the wedding seems like the Good Housekeeping Seal of Approval. How could I give the Good Housekeeping Seal of Approval to the murder of my friend?"

My father pushed himself unsteadily to his feet. He hadn't used his cane when he wheeled the cart in, but he used it now. He shuffled to the door, listened with a hand theatrically cupped to his ear, and shuffled back. It was a slow trip. He sat down right beside me this time. The smell of his lavender aftershave curdled my stomach. I felt trapped in the sagging bed.

"Son, I'm going to tell you something absolutely secret."

"Let me run take a shower real quick."

My father grimaced. He had two different colors of teeth. "Guatemala in the '50s was hot, hot, hot. The Reds controlled the unions, the university, half the army. The president, Arbenz, drank nothing but Russian vodka. We're talking early '50s. Before you were born. The powers that be sent me down here to douse the fire. Me and John Puerefoy. Pistol-packing Puerefoy—guess who coined that moniker." My father proudly pointed a thumb at himself in case I couldn't guess.

"Anyway, it was a very successful operation. We jammed the government radio station and set up our own guy broadcasting from the roof of the YMCA. They never caught him. We had planes dropping leaflets on every street corner. It was beautiful.

Everyone expected a huge invasion. Hell, they expected the Second Coming."

My father licked his lips. His cheeks glowed red. He leaned even closer and lowered his voice. "I was seeing quite a bit of Hoover then. He moved in the best circle. There were all kinds of women, but your mother was back in Virginia Beach and I was loyal. I resisted temptation right and left. But at the end, when Arbenz fell, the whole country went wild. You wouldn't believe the parties. There was total jubilation among the people."

"The rich people," I said.

"Don't kid yourself," my father said. "Everybody was turned on. It was revolution. Liberation. And there was this one woman. The ultimate on-fire creature. She'd danced with Che Guevara. She adored Americans." My father cleared his throat. He loosened his grip on the cane in his lap. "She was nineteen years old. I decided that the fruits of life are meant to be tasted. And I've never second-guessed myself." He glared at me fiercely, as if I'd better not challenge him. "The woman was Connie Montenegro. Marlón, by all accounts, is our blood."

Calmly, with just the right amount of fumbling, my father rummaged in his pockets for his meerschaum pipe, his alligator-skin tobacco pouch. The casual way he extracted a fat pinch of tobacco and tamped it down conveyed complete command. When he lit the pipe, flushed cheeks indrawn with each triumphant puff, it signified success, like Red Auerbach's victory cigar. My father loved the Boston Celtics. He loved all the perennial champs. The Green Bay Packers. The New York Yankees. Until they stopped winning. He hated the Boston Red Sox because they always eventually lost.

I was in shock. I had too many thoughts at once. Victory cigar. The phrase *to blow smoke*. My heart swelled like a balloon about to pop. It crossed my hyper mind that my father could have been a superstar in silent movies. His gestures and expressions seemed scaled for the big screen. But the talkies would have ended his career. He laid the sincerity on too thick.

"Does Mom know?" I asked.

"Your mother can sniff out sex better than a bloodhound. It's her keenest sense. I mean I came home so lovey-dovey. I came home so sweet. She bought it at first. In fact, that had to be when you were conceived. But I'll never forget the third night. She woke me up and shined the bedside light in my face and said: 'Who was she?' That was the first time I moved into the den."

I looked at the wicker blinds blocking the window. I toyed with the impulse to jump out the window and run. I didn't trust my father, but I didn't doubt him. "Hoover knows?" I said.

"Hoover knew before I did. He wrote me a nice long letter. He handled the situation."

"He married her," I said. "Your frat bro bailed you out when you knocked up his girlfriend."

"Connie was not Hoover's girlfriend. She was his dream. He worshipped the pot she pissed in. Hell, he worshipped the pot *I* pissed in."

My father chomped on his pipe as if to ruminate on the strangeness of Hoover. I brought my hands out from under the covers—from the defensive, secure, crotch-holding position—and clasped them against my chest. I recognized my father as a master tactician, a black belt in bullshit, and I refused to be out-maneuvered.

"Enough ancient history," he abruptly said. "The point is that Hoover wants into our family. Don't ask me why. To tell you the truth, I don't particularly want him in our family. But if you're going to marry his daughter, marry her right. Okay? Okay."

My father relit his pipe and held it to my lips. The ceremonial peace pipe. A clammy chill gripped the back of my neck. I realized that whatever I did might be exactly what my father intended. Even if I ditched Magdalena, it might be because he finessed me into it. When I gritted my teeth and shook my head, I was just getting another refusal out of my system, as far as he was concerned. He puffed on the pipe to his heart's content.

"I drank a real cup of coffee this morning," he said with a grin. "I ate a real egg. And this smoke is the first I've tasted since the last attack."

He drummed his fingers lightly against the bowl of the pipe. His manicured fingers. Red knuckles. Liver spots. His hands were smaller than mine but similarly active, similarly quick. They trembled a little. My father, however devious, however cunning, was an old man. And his hands, to me, meant something inexpressible.

I must have made my decision while I was looking at his hands. I'd take Magdalena to the Sheraton, we'd stay the weekend in separate rooms, and get married on Monday in front of a justice of the peace. But first I needed to placate my father. Or I needed to placate myself.

"I hate to let you down," I said. "I really do. Because I understand you a lot better than you think. I mean I love you. In spite of your weaknesses. In spite of your mistakes. We just have different values. That's all." I kissed his cheek. "Now why don't I go jump in the shower and you tell Hoover that you tried your best?" My father didn't move. I swung my legs out of the bed and sat naked beside him. "Maybe Magdalena and I'll come see you in a few weeks. How's that for a plan?"

My father grabbed me by the scruff of the neck. I shivered. It was the same cold touch I'd just imagined.

"In this world," he said, "you have to do things you don't want to do. That's maturity. Which you ain't got."

"I'm sorry, Dad. I really am."

"You've always been a fuck-up. Someday you'll outgrow it. You will. I can see it in your mouth. You're more selfish than anything else."

I broke his grip by standing. The oppressive stillness in the room threatened to immobilize both of us. "I have to do what I think is right," I said.

My father cracked the heavy head of the cane against my knee. He swung from the sitting position, but he put the full strength of his arms and chest into it. He grunted as he swung, as if he was playing tennis. I just gaped at him, until he swung again, connected again. I settled to the floor. Rocked back and forth, holding my knee.

"Different values, my ass," my father said. "There's nothing I've done that you won't do just as bad. Or worse. So show some respect." He jabbed the cane in my direction. "You cost me a daughter once. You cost me a daughter because you didn't follow my orders. This time you'll do as I say."

I looked up at my father with my mouth open. No words came. I was eight years old when my sister died. Eight.

"You're my blood," he said. "You owe me for life."

I suppose I could have snatched the cane away from him. It would have been physically possible. But I was stunned by his conviction. The tenacity of his will.

"Mary Alice was not my fault," I said, but I said it without strength.

"You were young," my father said. "Your judgment was poor. Your judgment is *still* poor. But we'll take care of that. Hoover spoke to Magdalena earlier this morning. She's ready to go along." He clamped his pipe between his false teeth and his real teeth. He smirked at me, semi-crumpled on the floor. I'd expected my nakedness to intimidate him. Some intimidation. While he dictated the unfavorable terms of my surrender, I pulled a sheet off the bed and covered up.

"You should thank me for this," he said at the end. I remembered saying the same thing to Armando. Sounding just as positive. I wondered when I'd sound that positive again.

My father—bless his heart muscle—handed me his cane on the way out. "Keep it," he said. "You may need it."

I gave him the finger. Behind his back. Was I macho or what?

XIX

MONSTER WEDDING

It so happens I grow tired of being a man.

PABLO NERUDA

Of my many superstitions the most powerful is this: I believe that nothing ever happens the way I expect. Sometimes I imagine the worst on purpose simply to prevent it. Do you do that? Or do you think positive? Or pray? We must feel safer practicing a system, even if it fails from time to time, because it extends the slim possibility that we control events, or at least exercise some influence.

Waking up Saturday morning with more aches than the day before, I imagined a magnificent cathedral. I imagined Spoon forcing the wedding ring onto Magdalena's thin finger while the parents signed the cross. "It could happen," I said out loud, as if saying so would protect us all.

After a scalding/freezing shower and a shave with a new blade, I laid out what was left of my belongings: khaki shorts, Hawaiian shirt, underwear, socks, handkerchiefs, mace, a bundle of dirty clothes, airline ticket, travel iron, dark blue suit. It was shorts weather, warm and humid, but I put on the suit and packed everything else into the burlap sack. Just to be on the safe side, I rechecked the closet and the chest of drawers, and then I slung the sack over my shoulder and ventured downstairs.

Connie was in full command, telling workmen where to put tables, instructing maids how tablecloths should hang, lecturing the caterer about olives.

"Green. Not black. I would never in a million years have ordered black." She turned to Spoon's mother, Adele, and explained in English: "Bad olives."

I managed to elbow the burlap sack behind my back before they caught sight of me.

Connie kissed my cheek and fiddled with my hair. Her

charm switched on, as if I deserved special consideration merely for being a male of the species.

"How do you say 'balm' in English?" Connie asked. "Poor Adele won't let me do a thing for her migraine."

Spoon stooped in front of the low mirror, adjusting his lopsided bow tie.

"It's a black day in Dallas," he said.

He pulled the knot loose and started over while I fought off the sensation of falling. My stomach cramped.

"Don't give me a hard time," he said. "Just put it on, okay?" He jerked his thumb at the tuxedo hanging from the closet door. "I had a marvelous chat with my father this morning. We worked out an incredibly fair compromise. Not only do we get to wear black armbands, the boldest of fashion statements, but my future brother-in-law has agreed to present himself to his deputy chief for a full and impartial whitewash of the murder of Hércules. Renews my faith in mankind, know what I mean?"

"Have you talked to Magdalena?" I said.

"Now that would be bad luck, wouldn't it?"

He stared at his fumbling hands in the mirror. I plodded around the bed and stood next to him for a second. His color was poor, a seasick shade of green, and his hands refused to steady. There was nothing to do but try on the tuxedo, which, despite contoured shoulders and an adjustable waistband, fit like a circus tent.

"Well, it's great to feel petite," I said.

"Do me a favor and screw the bright side," Spoon said. "Just this once."

A clatter from the ballroom punctuated the silence between us. Spoon yanked off his bow tie and used it to mop his temples. I opened the window as wide as it would go, but the air was just as hot outside and just as still.

"Would you tie my tie?" I said. I positioned myself in front of him at the mirror, his thumbs touching my throat.

"You want to know why," he said. "But you won't ask. You'd rather accuse me with those Bambi eyes." He looped a perfect, straight, symmetrical bow and tightened it around my neck. "I wish I had killed Marlón. Then I could get married with pride. Now it's like cutting my losses."

"That's a bad reason," I said, and immediately wished I hadn't. "I mean, you have better reasons than that."

"Yeah, I have reasons. But what do you have? You look like a clown in that monkey suit."

I glanced over my shoulder at his red-rimmed eyes. "I guess I kind of thought you could use the company."

"Bless you, Saint Armando."

I sat down on the edge of the bed next to his father's cane. I squeezed my sore feet into the glossy rented dress shoes with three-inch platform soles. I should have said right then that my feelings were hurt, but instead I asked a fretful question. "Would you rather I bowed out?"

His back stiffened. "You're just itching for an excuse," he said to my reflection in the mirror.

"No, sir," I said. "I'm your best man. Wedding or not."

His shoulder blades twitched. His whole body shook but he didn't turn around. "You're such a fucking mule," he said. "Your only power is to refuse. You quit law school, you quit marriage, and now you want to quit this. Well, I can't kill my father the way you killed yours."

My breathing stopped. I felt impossibly heavy and tired. I realized that I had been riding on adrenaline for days and that it must have run dry. I willed myself to go to Spoon, to put my leaden hand on his tense back. He swung his elbow into my neck.

"What's wrong?" I said. "Tell me what's wrong."

He whirled on me, or tried to whirl, but his leg buckled. He grabbed the bedpost for support.

"Are you okay?" I said.

He seized the cane and swiped at me close enough to raise the hairs on my wrist. His expression was terrible. I retreated almost into the closet.

"Out," he said. "Now." He jabbed the cane at the door.

"I at least need to change," I said.

He tapped the tip of the cane against the soft haunch of the bed while I undressed. I figured he couldn't hate me in my underwear. I figured if I took long enough, he'd repent. I lingered over the buttons of my shirt, tied my shoes in a double knot. I hung up the tuxedo and was starting to cover it with the plastic bag when he swung the cane against the bedpost, two vicious backhand whacks, and then, cocking the cane like a baseball bat, he did something I'd never seen him do before: he resisted an impulse. He stopped himself mid-swing. His whole body trembled. His mouth twisted into an unnatural grin. "It's the blood," he said, less to me than to some invisible judge. "The fucking crude McGuffin blood."

"Please," I said. "I'm your friend."

He brandished the cane as if to strike. Maybe I should have let him—I'd already licked boots and rolled in excrement—but I scrambled over the bed to the safety of the doorway.

"I'm your brother," I said. "I love you."

"Suck my dick," he said. He limped to the mirror and began to tie his tie again.

The burlap sack with my airline ticket lay on the bed. I decided after considerable deliberation to leave it. I trudged down the hall, across the hectic ballroom. Connie and Adele were perfecting an arrangement of flowers. The lower layers of the wedding cake sweated on a side table. No one paid me any particular attention, not even Pepito. I dragged myself outside and just kept on, step after sluggish step. I had no idea where to go. My stomach was empty, but I didn't feel like eating. I didn't feel like anything. A pallid haze hung motionless over the monumental houses, the cardboard shacks. The sky seemed to be holding its breath. There was no relief from the heat, no conceivable reason for Spoon's change of heart. I couldn't think, and I couldn't not think. Spoon had accused me of killing my father. He'd swung at me with a cane. All the explanations I constructed collapsed. Now and then I noticed a soldier or a family of Indians on the busy Saturday streets. Heat lightning flashed in the sky to the south. Maybe he needed to suffer without me, to bring on the worst possible disaster and endure it alone, to plummet unrestrained by any pretense of friendship. No, that described my brand of self-destruction, not his. The sound of the noon church bells filled me with a familiar sadness, each rich note mingling hope and regret.

A short while later, when I found myself at the taxi stand across from the central market, I couldn't believe that I'd had a destination. And yet there I was, asking directions to the Church of the Most Precious Blood, my voice as steady and calm as if I'd worked out this plan with shrewd logic beforehand.

A taxi driver automatically ushered me to his taxi. He refused to accept the fact that I was broke.

"Aren't you a *yanqui*?" he said.

"A *yanqui* without money," I said.

"*No existe,*" he said. He drew me a map on the back of a candy wrapper.

The wedding was scheduled for one-thirty; I had no desire to confront anyone; I dawdled along the well-marked route, reciting a poem by Pablo Neruda. It was an oddly literary thing to do. I turned more and more inward. I watched my feet crunch against the rough pavement. I felt the heat rise through the thin soles of my shoes. And at the same time, I began to compose sentences to describe my experience: "Armando Santiesteban was wet with sweat. Only his mouth was dry." Suddenly, I had the sense that here, in this foreign country, in this act of choosing words, I was coming face to face with myself, and that the distance between the two of me, the distance of self-consciousness, was reconciled by words. I *needed* to tell the story of this trip. Only the story would bridge the distance.

I passed the Church of the Most Precious Blood in a state of melancholy exhilaration. An elegant threesome was chatting in the scant shade of the entranceway. An old drunk in a panama hat was vehemently directing traffic. The boy soldiers on the corner looked me over without meeting my eyes.

A few blocks farther on, at a housefront store, I leaned over the counter to order a soda before it hit me that I didn't have a cent. Against my better judgment I asked for a glass of water, which I nursed along, amoeba by amoeba, until I realized that the grandfather clock in the corner must be permanently stuck.

I rushed back to the church, but I was still early. Dozens of wedding guests milled on the steps, fluttering fans and handkerchiefs. Almost everyone seemed to belong to Hoover's generation. Their powerful automobiles, double-parked on both sides of the street, clashed with the shabby neighborhood. The church itself wasn't shabby, but it was modest, except for its exotic Byzantine doorway. Crouched between a BMW and a Lincoln, I pictured Spoon and Magdalena emerging from that turnip-shaped doorway as man and wife.

The longer I waited, the more confused I became. As the first wave of guests surged into the church, I caught myself whistling a song from my wife's favorite movie, the scene where the neurotic hero crashes the wedding of the woman he loves and spirits her away. I covered my mouth. Of course I had no intention of running off with the bride—Spoon was the hero, not me—but I did have the potential, and with the potential came a certain sobering responsibility.

The steps emptied. My fingernails were in my mouth and I was chewing them. Inside the church a choir began to sing a traditional hymn. Why couldn't I go sit under a shade tree in the Parque Central? I remembered what my mother used to say to coax me to fox-trot or eat liver or do any disagreeable chore: "Give yourself a chance to like it." I didn't make a conscious decision. My heavy body just crossed the street and climbed the steep stone steps.

The heat inside the church had reached steam-bath intensity. Out of the murky gloom scuttled an old woman in a pillbox hat who pressed a packet of rice against my sweaty palm.

"Friend of the groom," I said guiltily.

A side door creaked open, and all of a sudden Magdalena and Hoover were advancing toward me, heads lowered, their progress as slow and smooth and inexorable as a glacier's. Magdalena wore a veil that revealed only a dark suggestion of downcast eyes and pinched mouth. Nothing hid Hoover's grim expression, the furtive pride of an executioner. I braced myself for a collision, but they veered to the threshold of the main aisle. I edged up behind them as close as the length of her train. I don't know what I expected to hear—the last desperate plea of the sacrificial virgin?—but instead, as the choir segued into a series of soaring arpeggios, Hoover kissed Magdalena lightly on the ear and whispered what sounded like "I love you with all my soul." If she had squirmed or struggled or shown any outward sign of revulsion, maybe I would have tried something extreme. Instead, Hoover solemnly said "Geronimo" as if it were their private joke and she let him steer her down the aisle to the opening strains of the processional.

I tottered to the far end of the last row and knelt. I hadn't set foot inside a church since my father's funeral. The words of Psalm 42 formed on my lips as the priest spoke them: "Do me justice, O God, and fight my fight against a faithless people." I'd served as an altar boy until I was past thirteen. I'd enjoyed the ritual and the repetition, the robes and the incense, the meticulous attention to detail. In fact, my priest, Father Vickers, often asked me to consider the priesthood. He was a quick-tempered alcoholic. The other boys called him Whisky Sour. The day they all quit to join Pony League, they left a bottle of mouthwash on the altar. I didn't exactly worship Father Vickers, but I hated to disappoint him. I waited to turn in my surplices until he went to Lake Tahoe on his annual Fourth of July vacation. That same night my father stood in the light of my bedroom doorway with his hands clasped behind his back. "You did it," he said softly.

"The priest had such bad breath," I said.

My father broke into a laugh, the hardest I ever remember him laughing. "Thank God that priest don't drink vodka instead of gin." My father presented me with a gift still in the bag from the store, a baseball glove autographed by Luis Aparicio. The price tag was scraped off, but I knew exactly how much it cost. It was the most expensive gift he ever gave me, except for the leather briefcase he bought after I was accepted to law school.

"Lord have mercy," the priest said. "Christ have mercy."

The priest's high, warbly voice came through speakers mounted between the stained-glass stations of the cross. A microphone dropped on a long green cord from the cross beam above the altar, as did two mysterious boxes decorated with flowery vines. This priest enunciated much more clearly than Father Vickers, as if he were concentrating on the literal meaning of the prayers. I recognized him as the serene monsignor from the engagement party at Casa Schultz, the enthusiastic collector of Quixotes. His immense white forehead glowed like a crystal ball.

Spoon and Magdalena stood before him, mismatched by size and posture at the very least. She held herself as steadfastly as a toy bride atop a cake, back perfectly arched, shoulders perfectly straight, even her elbows perfect. He leaned against his father's cane, adjusted his armband, tugged his unruly red hair.

The armband infuriated me. It was such a weak protest, a token rebellion, which suddenly seemed typical of Spoon. I wanted him to jump up on the altar and scream the name of Hércules. But the armband relieved him of further obligation. It signified the hero he would no longer be.

He was floundering up there. He didn't have a plan. He wasn't waiting for the perfect moment to act. I realized that in spite of my efforts to expect the worst, I'd clung to the most foolish hope. I'd maintained a glimmer of faith in Spoon — until now. Now when he turned around, when he twisted his long, scrawny, vulnerable neck, I ducked. I knew he was looking for help and I knew there was nothing I could do. My only power was to refuse. He'd said so himself.

The monsignor poured the wine into the chalice. The assisting priest poured the water. I crossed my arms against my chest and breathed deep.

". . . O Lord, set a sentinel before my mouth, a guard at the door of my lips. Let not my heart engage in deeds of wickedness. . . ."

The monsignor passed the censer over the bread and wine with delicacy and precision, every wisp of incense precious. Even the washing of the fingers he performed with exuberant reverence. Father Vickers had always appeared to sleepwalk through Mass. "We are instruments of the Lord," he'd told the altar boys. "We must surrender to His will in a holy trance." The monsignor, on the other hand, actively interpreted the rituals. He murmured the secret prayers in an anguished undertone, as if they contained truths too unbearable to be pronounced.

My only power was to refuse.

Suddenly it seemed as though nothing significant had happened since the last time I was in church, the stifling September afternoon of my father's funeral. The years in between flattened out like a valley between barren peaks. It was just an illusion, a trick of perspective, but it suggested how little I'd really changed.

I'd refused to carry my father's coffin. I'd refused even to look at his corpse. "Go see him," my mother had said. "He's resting easy. Give yourself a chance to forgive." I'd gritted my teeth and clenched my fists, determined to show nothing, to feel nothing, while she'd cried into her hands. When she'd touched her warm tears to my dry cheeks, dabbing them on like paint or makeup, I'd sat tight. I'd swallowed everything.

What was different now? I was even wearing the same suit, my battle suit, Spoon and Betsy used to call it, because I'd donned it like armor for every law school interview, every formal social function, every third workday of my summer internships. Back then I'd identified with the suit: sensible, durable, practical, your basic blue. Now I regretted its stodginess, its lack of style. One cuff was badly frayed. The sleeves were shiny at the elbow. *The worse for wear,* I said out loud. I pitied myself. I saw my life as a series of failures, the same indefinable failure repeated over and over again.

I remembered the night I told my father, the night I told him I needed a break. That was exactly how I thought of it at the time. I needed a break, from law school, from marriage, just for a little while, until I felt ready to go on. I'd found him at the ballpark watching my brother's Little League game, enjoying the loyal company of his Styrofoam beer cooler. He'd smiled his thin smile and passed me a beer. We drank without talking for a few innings. He was in a decent mood. He liked it when we drank and didn't talk. "I may find a place in San Francisco for a month or two," I said. "Just kind of unwind."

My father shrugged; kept his eyes on the game.

"The whole lawyer deal—I need a break. Betsy understands."

My father downed the dregs of his beer. "A man's got to do what a man's got to do," he said. It was probably his favorite stock expression. He opened his free hand all the way and slowly clenched it into a fist. "They treat you bad out there?" he asked. He sounded interested for once.

"They treat me fine. Maybe too fine. I mean you wouldn't believe the money they spend. My firm took all twenty summer associates to Cape Cod for the weekend. A retreat, they called it, but it was nothing like Father Vickers. Beautiful fancy food, wine by the year. This one partner kept slapping me five, giving me the high five as if that was what I could relate to. You know what he said to me? He said: 'We need a good young Hispanic on our team.' You just don't feel like you belong sometimes. The only other Hispanic works in the mail room. I mean, let's face it. I'm a paperboy from Reedley."

My father leaned across the cooler and thumped me on the chest. "They're no better than you."

"That's what I'm afraid of. I wish they were better. Then maybe they'd deserve all that money, all that success. They act like they deserve it. No one *deserves* it."

"Why not?" My father squinted at me. His face tightened into something hard. "Why not you raking in the bucks? You don't have to be a saint. One saint in the family is enough."

"I don't know. My mind is all screwed up right now. I need a break."

"It's your life," my father said. He wiped his nose with his thumb and forefinger. He pulled the tab on another beer. When his nose started really running, I gave him a handkerchief. That was the best I could do for him. I was too wrapped up in my own troubles to put myself in his situation: a forty-nine-year-old man with kidneys so bad he couldn't drive a truck anymore, he had to make a living stocking produce at the local chain supermarket, he had to wear a red apron and a name tag. Both my parents wore name tags. While I lived in dread of the name tag with my name on it. I helped my father finish the beer. We carried the empties home in the Styrofoam cooler. I wouldn't realize how much I'd disappointed him until he was dead.

The bell tinkled three times. "My Lord and My God." The monsignor elevated the chalice of sacramental wine become the blood of Christ. I couldn't watch. Transubstantiation, like heaven, had always seemed far-fetched to me. I only believed in the negative concepts: sin, guilt, eternal damnation.

I stared off at the stained-glass stations of the cross, the lurid El Greco colors darkening as the sky outside darkened. A pair of ogre-ish Roman soldiers cruelly prodded Christ along. They swaggered, they sneered, they exuded contempt, in exaggerated contrast to Christ's rhapsodic bliss. I disliked the cartoon aspect—the naive caricature of evil versus good—but I was held by the powerful tension between the figures. The ogres needed the martyr and vice versa. In the third panel, where one of the soldiers casually kicked Christ as He fell, Christ's expression verged on the ecstatic, as if He took pleasure, perverse pleasure, in His own suffering. Or perhaps the perverse pleasure was mine.

Then Spoon was shaking his head. The monsignor stood over him, proffering the holy wafer.

"May the body of our Lord Jesus Christ preserve your soul to life everlasting," the monsignor said.

Spoon refused communion, wagging his head like a cantankerous child. The monsignor coughed. The assisting priest coughed with him.

The monsignor bent forward and whispered to Spoon, who nodded yes for several seconds and then shook his head no. The monsignor coughed again, a dry, scratchy, throat-scraping cough. His face turned blotchy red all the way up to the hairline. The vine-covered boxes on each side of the altar stirred with the fluttering of agitated birds.

It was one of those rare public moments when the order of things is disrupted and freedom exists, however briefly. Hoover motioned the monsignor over to the altar and slapped him on the back, but the coughing persisted. An altar boy rushed from the sacristy with a bottle of Fanta Orange, which the monsignor sipped, haltingly, while Hoover whispered into his ear. Everyone else remained kneeling—except Spoon and his father. They stood toe to toe, jawing at each other. Spoon gripped his father by the shoulders; his father gripped Spoon by the arms. They swayed out of rhythm, like a pair of dubious dancers, both accustomed to having the lead.

I got up off my knees. The heat pressed against me like a

damp sponge. Simply to breathe, to fill the lungs with sufficient air, demanded a huge effort. I tightroped up the side aisle, past a dusty case filled with antique jewelry, flickering devotional candles, scraps of paper scribbled with prayers. I gathered in the wild hope of all those prayers, the hope for no less than a miracle. I waved at Spoon, but he didn't see me. He was still grappling with his father. From where I stopped, a few rows from the front, I couldn't determine how much force either was exerting. Spoon squirmed, but Spoon always squirmed. He might have been trying to break loose, but he might have been hanging on tight.

I waved. I fluttered my handkerchief.

Meanwhile, Hoover finished with the monsignor and charged Spoon and his father. He clamped down on both of them. The microphone picked up an occasional harsh sibilant and broadcast it throughout the hushed church. Spoon's father knelt almost meekly, but Spoon twisted and jerked.

And that was when he finally caught sight of me, ineffectually waving my white handkerchief, just as he sank to the floor. A frightful grin distorted his mouth. I wanted to inspire him, I wanted a ray of golden light to shine between us, but my show of solidarity fell flat. He must have seen in my eyes what I saw in his: the reflection of doubt.

He turned to the altar. Hoover let go of him, tentatively, the way you'd let go a quavering house of cards. His shoulders drooped in surrender. His heavy head tilted to the side, toward Magdalena, his resolute bride-to-be, who had remained quite still during the commotion. She'd maintained her elegant bearing despite whatever torments seized her heart. I couldn't help recognizing her strength, its source as familiar as my shadow. Denial supported her achingly taut back. Denial placed her hand in Spoon's.

The monsignor resumed his position above them. His face had lost its color. His voice sluggish and thick, he led Spoon in an act of Spiritual (rather than Holy) Communion:

> *My Jesus, I believe that You are in the*
> *Blessed Sacrament. I love You above all*
> *things and I long for You in my soul.*

Since I cannot now receive You sacramentally,
come at least spiritually into my heart. I
embrace You and unite myself entirely to
You; never permit me to be separated from You.

And so Spoon dodged the holy wafer. He protected some ves-
tige of his honor, in his own mind at least. Magdalena received
the sacrificial banquet with a graceful nod. Spoon's father followed, shuffling to the railing, creaking to his knees, shrinking,
or appearing to shrink, inside his wrinkled linen jacket soaked
with sweat at the shoulder blades. Everyone took communion:
Hoover, Connie, a procession of well-groomed women and
men, each the same, each different: shy, mechanical, exultant,
bemused. It occurred to me as I looked on from the safe distance of the side aisle that the bride and groom were not the
real center of attention here; they faced the altar just like everyone else, their vows would constitute only a small portion of
these proceedings, and, in fact, they provided no more than an
excuse for this ceremony, this ceremony with nearly two thousand years of momentum. How could I presume to interfere, I
asked myself. It wasn't my way to presume.

The Mass went on. I joined in the recitation of the Lord's
Prayer. There would be no miracle, no transcendent heroic act,
and yet I breathed easy for a change. Believe it or not, I felt the
flush of accomplishment. Wasn't I less of a wreck now than
when my father died? Back then I couldn't conceive of moving;
just now I had moved. Even my drastic mood swings seemed
like an improvement. Normally, I hovered near the middle of
the emotional spectrum. I was like the viola in an orchestra. The
viola would never hit notes as high as the violin or as low as the
cello, but it had its own register with its own limited richness.
Ever since I'd set off with Sonny's package, it was as if I were
hitting notes far beyond my range.

Spoon fidgeted while the monsignor washed the holy chalice. He pressed the cane against the back of his neck during
Final Prayers. At first he held the cane like a barbell and then,
abjectly or not, he hung his arms over it as if it were a cross.

Wait, I wanted to say. The big martyr is not *you*. I thought
I saw through Spoon's tasteless crucifixion pose. He was

mocking himself, making himself ridiculous, because he'd failed Hércules. You didn't invent failure, I wanted to say. Learn to do better. Let life teach you compromise.

I bowed my head and remembered how Spoon had accused me. "I can't kill my father the way you killed yours." The charge seemed so obviously unfounded. I hadn't killed my father. I wasn't that powerful. My father had driven too fast on a dark road under the influence of more than he could handle. After a long accumulation of disappointments, failures, and defeats, he hit something too hard, with too little protection, and it killed him.

While Spoon and Magdalena, on their knees, repeated the archaic incantations of betrothal, I took off my father's cross and draped it over the pew in front of me. I tapped it lightly and watched it swing. My father had carved the cross himself from a knotty chunk of scrub oak, on a rain-spoiled day at Lake Nacimiento. To avoid the family jigsaw puzzles, the endless games of dominoes and tiddlywinks, he'd painted the cross with three meticulous coats of my sister Dolores's hot-pink nail polish. She'd screamed because he'd ruined the tiny applicator brush. I heard Spoon and Magdalena promise each other the impossible, but I was more interested in the cross, its nicks and gouges where the polish had chipped off. The monsignor invoked the awesome threat of the Almighty—"What God hath joined together let no man put asunder"—Magdalena lifted her veil, and Spoon kissed her, their foreheads bumping, their misparted lips not quite finding the ideal fit.

As if to distract us from this awkwardness, the choir sang "Jesu, Joy of Man's Desiring." The altar boy released two swarms of white birds from the camouflaged cages above the altar. The young voices of the choir achieved an effortless sweetness. The frenzied wingbeat of more than a dozen semisuffocated doves lent the music a truly Guatemalan rhythm.

Spoon, with Magdalena's support, hobbled on his cane down the aisle. He looked determined, negotiating each short difficult step, surprisingly determined, as if he still might be plotting to save the world, eventually.

It seemed possible, as the birds soared and swooped, that he might be getting what he wanted by pretending not to want it. Magdalena squeezed his arm. He kept his eyes aimed straight ahead. I wished them well together before I turned my back and idly spun my father's cross around my finger.

The monster wedding was over. The marriage was on. While I waited for the tide of guests to go out, a dove settled on the pew in front of me and preened its wings. The altar boy trooped across the altar with a long wooden pole like the one I'd used as window monitor in elementary school. I happened to glance up at the last station of the cross, and there was Christ, no longer beatific or even resigned, but suffering, agonizing, His face transfixed by pain and fear, like a real dying man. And the Roman soldier who had kicked Him looked identical, as if he were suffering the same pain. I sniffed my father's cross. It had always smelled like rain to me, but now it smelled like the fire in the Mission the night of my thirtieth birthday. I decided to leave the cross here in the church, as proof that I had changed.

What do you call it when your life seems to make sense? I call it an illusion, because the sense dissolves so quickly, the way dreams dissolve once you realize you're dreaming. Nevertheless, when I slapped the cross down on the seat of the pew, my life seemed to make sense, and I was grateful. I might have marched from the church full of new confidence, but the altar boy distracted my attention, poking one of the cages with his pole. He tipped the cage to a sharp angle and jiggled the pole until a dove fell out, a fat, stiff dove whose wings flared a little, but not enough to slow the fall. The altar boy shook the dove gently, as if it were a lightbulb that might or might not be defective. Then he snapped the dove's neck, hiked up his cassock, and stuffed the dove headfirst down his pants.

And just like that my life went back to not making sense. Not only is the worst always worse than you expect, it's less dignified, more unwieldy, fuller of estrangement.

I followed the last of the stragglers outside, where the sky had turned a suffocating shade of purple. Hoover's Mercedes pulled away from the curb, replaced by a dented limo. The drunk in the panama hat had taken charge. He ceremoniously swung the door open for Spoon's parents, who thanked him with a damp bill he tucked in his hatband as he whistled for the next vehicle. He conducted traffic like a dervish, stomping his feet, pumping his arms, guiding each passenger with an effusive pat. I longed for such guidance. I longed to slip into a car and ride.

The maestro loped up to help a man in a wheelchair, the colonel who had chanted "*Vi-no, vi-no,*" at the engagement party at Casa Schultz. "Careful, imbecile," the colonel yelled, but the maestro never slowed down. "A few good bumps are healthy for a man," he said. "Pretend you're on top of a beautiful woman." He plopped the colonel into his Imperial and blew a kiss to the colonel's unperturbed wife.

It wasn't a bad moment to leave on, but I couldn't leave. I lingered at the top of the steps, puzzling over my options. The choirboys were rolling cigarettes with waxy yellow papers and the blackest tobacco. If they'd offered me a cigarette, I probably would have taken one. I was that open to suggestion.

When the altar boy came around the side of the church, rumpled tail feathers of the dove protruding from his back pocket, I started after him. I can't explain why. Maybe the only reason was that I didn't have a reason. I wanted to go on instinct. I wanted to explore the unknown streets of the city, discover the unknown lives, for no reason at all. At the bottom of the steps, though, I stopped. Something felt wrong. I had a paralyzing attack of self-consciousness, as if I'd caught sight of myself in a mirror. Who was I fooling? I was a cautious, deliberate, rational person. I needed reasons. The altar boy rounded the corner and was gone.

Later, I would retrace my path to the central market.

I would barter my battle suit for cooler clothes and place a collect call to my sister, who would graciously agree to wire $500 to the local American Express office.

I would find—after five tries—a *pensión* willing to extend credit to an undocumented Mexican American.

That night I would bum dinner at a crowded pizza parlor, scavenging the remains of other people's pizza.

The next day, Sunday, I would sleep.

Monday I would drop by American Express, the American Consulate, and National Police Headquarters.

Tuesday I would head for Santa Catalina and get so miserably sick I'd have to turn back in Antigua.

Wednesday and Thursday I would spend in a dank, windowless bathroom, contemplating the cracks in the cement floor and promising myself that if I survived the dreadful ordeal I would stay in Guatemala and write this account of my trip.

At that moment, though, stuck in front of the Church of the Most Precious Blood, I had no idea what to do. Soon the last cars drove off. The choirboys scattered, swapping amateurish curses. The old maestro in the panama hat smoothed the edges of his crumpled bills. Still, I couldn't leave. My suit was drenched with sweat. The air tasted sour, as if all the oxygen had been pumped out of it. I needed something, and because nothing else was obviously missing, I decided to go back for my father's cross. I just wanted a token of my experience, and besides, the pink, paint-chipped cross represented a force I believed in: the passage of time.

I mounted the steps toward the oddly curved doors that seemed more appropriate to a mosque than a Catholic church. I wondered who had chosen this church. Perhaps it was the only one available on short notice. The dark outline of the doors loomed before me. I didn't realize until the moment I passed through them that they were shaped like praying hands.

X X

HOT FLASHES

Mercy, mercy me.
Things ain't what
They used to be.
MARVIN GAYE

I come to you tonight with a heavy heart.

Mr. President, Mr. President.

Glad you asked that question, son. But as I was saying before I so rudely interrupted myself, there's only two things certain in this miserable world: death and taxes. In the case of Guatemala, it happens to be our taxes and their death. Fair? No. Advantageous to us? Hmm, yes, now that you mention it. But that's not the point. The point is the evil of drugs. The point is equal opportunity for all rich people everywhere, regardless of rape, greed, or killer. The point is Armando's ex-wife called last month and put me on a bummer. *Muy mal.* Seems Armando turned up missing, as it were.

But let me spill everyone else's beans first. Like in the movies when the credits roll and the music swells and a voice-over gives the update on all the stars and costars, one by one, each face filling the screen.

My father is still hanging on for mere life. His gonads are gone. His old brittle feet won't support his full weight. But his brain functions like a steel trap. The only bone of contention being who's trapped.

My mother continues to conduct her separate life in the same house as the old man. Same house, different rooms.

My brother hasn't mentioned his Miss Angel Flowers again, although he has been taking an unusual number of long business trips.

Hoover and Connie, those incorrigible romantics—who cares?

Marlón, like pond scum, has risen. To *capitán,* going on

caudillo. He'll never be punished for the murder of Hércules. It was just a career move for him, a résumé stuffer.

As for my beloved Magdalena, I successfully impregnated her on our honeymoon in Banff. She had a shaky first trimester, but now she swims a mile a day at the YWCA and her eyes, in unguarded moments, shine with an exultant light. Sometimes I imagine her abandoning me. She's already unfaithful, as far as I'm concerned. She lacks faith. I'll never forget our fiasco under the bola tree at La Esperanza. *That,* I'm afraid, was our defining moment. I fell at her feet and begged for a little love. She held back something fierce. The best part of our marriage is waking up together and describing our dreams. She dreams often of airports—my only clue to her inner life. I dream often of a certain gifted New Paultz girl in my Peoples of Mesoamerica seminar, but those dreams I keep to myself.

So. Anyway. I was in my office grading midterms when Betsy Fairbanks Santiesteban Weiss called and asked if I'd heard from Armando. I dug his package out of my file cabinet while she made a long story short. Fact was, Armando had neglected to come home. His mother was worried and the American Embassy was no help. I promised to do what I could, but I didn't do much until a week later when Betsy called again. In the mournful month since then, I've blown a thousand bucks on phone bills. I've talked to Hoover almost daily. I've talked to the Guatemalan Action Network. I've even talked to Marlón. I've had contacts with the police, the army, several newspapers, the secret police, the secret army, the Mutual Support Group, the Catholic church, the Guerilla Army of the Poor. . . . Armando was last seen in Santa Catalina. He arrived on foot, asked a few questions at the post office, and that was it. He hasn't shown up since. I'm afraid he's joined the ranks of the permanently disappeared.

Every party needs a pooper/that's why I invited myself.

Of course anything's possible. Hope springs eternal in the human breast. (Was that Shakespeare or "Casey at the Bat"?) But just the other night, I heard from the Guatemalan Action Network guy, who'd heard from his source in Panajachel, who'd spoken to the brother-in-law of the military commissioner in

San Blás, and evidently someone somewhere saw something (a cross the color of cheap lipstick wrapped around the branch of an oak tree), and the word now on Armando is forget about him.

Don't shoot the messenger. You wanted the facts, didn't you? My skin has the awful rubbery texture of a balloon. My head is banging so hard I had to shut off my Walkman. And then the refrigerator hum stopped. You know the hour before dawn is the deadliest? The hour more hearts give out, arteries clog, synapses snap? It's the silence that kills. The silence of betwixt and between. So I tuned in a talk show and set my headphones here on my desk. The muffled voices sound like judges from another planet. *These earthlings are sick.* That's what they're saying. Still, in a pinch, any voice is better than nothing—and I mean *nothing. Nada.* What darkness is a metaphor for.

Dawn is hype. Although Armando, I'm sure, would make this dawn inspirational. "A ribbon of pale light unwrapped the new day like the cellophane tab on a pack of cigarettes." Okay, okay. I do a lousy Armando. Which is why, now that I mention it, I've brought you here. *The murderer is in this room!* No. Wait. Wrong script. I've brought you here because Armando deserves a listen. One more time. In his own lugubrious words.

Can we share? When the department secretary brought me Armando's package, the Guatemalan stamps triggered hot flashes. It wasn't just the disturbing influence of Magdalena's vivid pregnancy books—the semester was barely beginning, my desk was already cluttered with unfinished paperwork, and the sight of Armando's perfect penmanship threw me for a loop. If the package had been addressed to anyone else, I'm sure I would have peeked inside, but it was mine to do with as I pleased, and I decided that as long as I didn't open it, I didn't have to tell Magdalena about it.

Fast forward to the first phone call from Armando's ex-wife.

The instant I recognized her voice—and she has a rich, warm, husky voice—my heart lost its grip. *Thumpkick, thumpkick.* Like a cat in a bag. I tore through my file cabinet, ripped open the package (all the while saying "uh-huh, uh-huh"), and frantically scanned Armando's letter, as if there might be reason to hurry. But I knew. I already knew. How should I put it? The letter came from the other side of the grave. And the concern in Betsy's voice. And my trite reassurances. "Don't worry. Armando's a big boy." While there on my desk, holding down a batch of blue books, lay my favorite wedding gift, Armando's canister of mace.

Wouldn't it be nice if he was on his way to Tierra del Fuego? Wouldn't it be nice if his story was published one day, in a decade or so, with the names changed to protect the guilt-ridden?

Whatever. In the spirit of Gandhi and Martin Luther King and Jimmy the Greek, it is indeed a great honor and rare privilege, blah blah blah. These are the words Armando left me with.

★ ★ ★

Dear Patrick,

For any offense I may have committed, for any failure as a friend, I'm sorry. I hope you and Magdalena are doing well. Please rest assured I hold no grudges—and if that sounds like a veiled accusation, I apologize again.

How's Connecticut? How do you like being a professor?

As I imagine you've figured out, I'm still in Guatemala. After the wedding I decided to stay and write the enclosed bundle of pages. I needed to tell the story of our trip, and I knew I'd never do it if I went back. Believe it or not, the prospect of typing tedious legal documents in my cubicle on the twenty-ninth floor held scant allure.

I used to read Dear Abby to my mother every morning while she made breakfast and bag lunches for my father and us kids. I'd follow her around the kitchen with the newspaper in my hand. If she got real interested, she'd stop and pour herself more coffee. "Read that last part over," she'd say. "That Dear Abby sure knows her stuff." One letter, I remember, seemed to appear again and again with only minor variations. A woman would write in about a man she'd met, a wonderful man in so many ways, except he picked his toes at the dinner table or drank or broke dishes or woke up in the middle of the night screaming. I want to marry him, Abby, the letter would say, but tell me if you think he'll change. Abby's answer was always the same: *they never change.* And my mother, in her red terry-cloth bathrobe and fluffy purple slippers, would sip her warmed-up coffee and sigh with the wisdom of her years. "They sure don't, dear. They don't ever change." Naturally, I believed her. How could I doubt my mother and Dear Abby? I couldn't—until this trip. The trip has changed me, or so I maintain, not that I've become assertive and slim and devil-may-care, but I hope I've shed a little of my self-preoccupation. I hope I've lost a little fear. Dear Abby was wrong. People do change. That's one reason I've written these pages. The other reasons are harder to explain.

You never let me tell you what happened when I tried to deliver Sonny Tzoc's package. The best description I can come up with is the line from the old limbo song: "How low can you go?" I went pretty damn low, but after all the false bottoms I've crashed through, it was almost a comfort to drop to my knees and grovel. Dignity was no longer an issue. I pleaded for life, and while I was pleading, I promised—promised *twice*—to tell the truth about Guatemala. I realize how grandiose that must sound, but during my awful confinement in the bathroom of the *Pensión Buena Vista,* I discovered that I felt an obligation. It was only food poisoning, but forty-eight hours of stomach cramps, diarrhea, and vomiting is as close to purgatory as I care to get. If not for three Salvadoran cousins who brought me bottled water and Pepto Bismol, I might have expired. God bless those cousins. They're probably working in a sweatshop in southern California by now, if they were able to sneak across the border.

I wish we could talk face to face. I've been thinking of you all day.

This morning while I was photocopying the manuscript, I met a young American girl. "You wrote all that?" she said. "Cool."

She explained what she was photocopying—a form letter to friends and relatives asking them to finance her trip to Tierra del Fuego—and asked if I'd care to donate to the cause.

She was dark and plump, almost owlish, with unshaved legs and armpits. She wore a tie-dyed halter top, quilted jeans skirt, Birkenstocks, a nose ring (!), and lots of political badges: Stop

Apartheid, the female symbol, Don't Eat Rain Forest Beef. What struck me most about her was her youth. I suppose you only recognize youth as a quality after you've lost it. She had youth.

"The worst sin is to give nothing because you can only give a little," she said. "I put that quote in my letter."

"I'll donate to breakfast," I said.

She introduced herself as Isadora. She said she'd graduated from high school a semester early and her parents had sent her down to Antigua to study Spanish. "I'm looking for someone stable to travel with," she said. "Someone as enlightened and politically aware as myself." In the middle of breakfast, she asked if I wanted to smoke a joint in her hotel room later.

You may have this kind of charged encounter every time you conduct office hours, but for me it was rare and racy. The only person I really talk to here is the proprietor of the *Buena Vista*, a retired photographer dying of cancer, and when Isadora asked me where I was from, I practically poured out the story of my life—and not just my past, but my future. Brace yourself, Patrick. My plan is to move back to the Central Valley and enroll in the bilingual education program at Fresno State. It's strange. Ever since I told the guerillas I was an elementary school teacher, I've wanted to make the lie true. I also want to work for the Sanctuary movement, and when I mentioned that to Isadora, she said, "Oh, yeah, the Sanctuary movement. Like the Underground Railroad during Prohibition."

I should have laughed. It's a funny image: black bottles of hooch hiding in basement after basement on their way north to freedom. But somehow I was terribly disappointed. And you were the only one I could think of who might understand why. Do you understand? I was disappointed because compared to the average American, Isadora probably *is* relatively enlightened, relatively aware. Nobody knows what's happening in the world.

I thought of our Abnormal Psychology class, your big debate with the uptight teaching assistant. Remember Snide Clyde? I bet he still has nightmares about you. He used to quiver every time you raised your hand. "McGuffin, McGuffin, what precious pearls of wisdom will you cast before us now?" That's how it started, I'm almost positive.

You brandished your textbook at him as if you'd found a misprint in a holy tablet. "Do you really believe that mass insanity is a valid diagnosis of the Third Reich?"

He wiped his granny glasses with the tip of his Brooks Brothers tie. "What do you mean by *valid,* McGuffin? Define your terms. Be precise."

"I mean *meaningful,*" you said. "Revealing. Not a cop-out."

"Cop-out?"

"A trick. A lie. To comfort ourselves. If they were insane, then we're okay. But if they were normal, if they were like us, then what are *we* capable of?"

"McGuffin, did you read the chapter or just look at the pictures? The notion here is delusion, societywide delusion."

"Isn't society a delusion?"

"What a terrifyingly original concept—for a high school sophomore."

"The citizens of Nazi Germany shared illusions and we don't?"

"We're not exterminating millions, no."

"Then it's the body count that counts, as far as you're concerned."

"No, but a qualitative distinction—"

"Fuck the qualitative distinction. If the North Vietnamese write the next textbook—if the subjugated people of Rhodesia or Watts write the next textbook—if there *is* a next textbook—will we seem saner than the guy who delivered milk in the town down the road from Dachau? Some guy delivered the milk. Some guy who didn't gas anybody. Was he a victim of mass insanity?"

"I'm afraid your argument is swallowing its own tail."

"The textbook sucks. Nobody acknowledges what's going on around here. Our whole society practices blindness. Willful blindness. It's stupid to pretend we're sane."

"In your case, McGuffin, that might be true. Why don't you write me an essay on the subject? To make up for your dreadful midterm."

He fixed you with the Snide Clyde glare; you flapped and flailed like a flightless bird. I was embarrassed to be sitting next to you. You were so obnoxious, so obviously in love with your own zeal. You found some good words, though. And I think I finally caught on to your frustration.

I tried to tell Isadora the story of the blindfolded peasant. "Suppose you had to shoot that peasant if you wanted to keep your Birkenstocks and your patchouli oil and your joints."

"My stuff is homegrown," she said. "Besides, I'm not into possessions."

By this time we'd finished not only breakfast but several cups of coffee. I wondered where my moral obligation lay. Should I try to convince her to go home? Or might she be better off heading south? You, I imagined, would have recommended a few of Tierra del Fuego's best bars and restaurants.

I miss you. I miss your messy life. It's funny, but until I finished this account of our trip, it was like you were still around. I practically smelled the mescal on your breath. Now I feel the distance between us.

It's nearly dawn here at the front desk of the *Buena Vista*. I'm the night man, you may be surprised to learn. The proprietor gives me a free room and a few quetzals a week to unlock the door for any carousers who straggle in after midnight. Occasionally, a guest drifts downstairs to complain about mosquitoes or confess his troubles, but usually I'm alone and it's quiet and I write. A week ago at this hour, I stopped writing for a minute, planted my elbows on the counter, and rested my chin in the cup of my hands. I may or may not have fallen asleep, but all of a sudden my chin slipped off my hands and when I looked up I saw a face suspended just on the periphery of my field of vision. It hung there, like a flesh-and-blood balloon, above my left shoulder. When I turned to look at it directly, it moved. I had to look by not looking. It was a man's face, a dark-skinned Guatemalan man wearing heavy black glasses, the lenses of which were shattered into tiny crystals, opaque but intact, concealing the eyes. The expression of the mouth hovered between despair and resignation. As soon as I recognized the face as Refugio's, it faded into the darkness.

Have you heard from him? I'm sure he reached home safely, but tomorrow I'm going up to Santa Catalina just to make sure. Isadora said she'd like to come along, but the truth is there's no one I'd rather travel with than you.

I hope we can get together soon. I have a reservation on a first-class bus to Mexico City in a few days, and from there I'll catch a bus to Tijuana. The Salvadoran cousins filled me in on the drill. Even if I stop in Reedley for a day or two, I should be back at work on the twenty-ninth floor by the time you receive this.

So write me a long letter. I'm assuming you'll let me know what you think of my efforts. All I can say is, you'd better. There are gaps in the story only you can fill in. Besides, I'd love to hear from you. Remember, you never regret the things you do, only the things you don't do.

Patrick, Spoon, friend, *hermano,* give my regards to Magdalena, and always, always consider me your brother.

Un abrazo,
Armando

The author wishes to acknowledge several works that broadened his understanding of Guatemala: *Campesino* and *Son of Tecún Umán* by Ignacio Bizarro Ujpán, translated and edited by James D. Sexton; *Bitter Fruit* by Stephen Schlesinger and Steven Kinzer; *Inevitable Revolutions* by Walter LeFeber; *Inverse Images* by John Hawkins; *I, Rigoberta Menchú* by Rigoberta Menchú, edited by Elisabeth Burgos-Debray and translated by Ann Wright; *Bird of Life, Bird of Death* by Jonathan Maslow; *Harvest of Violence* by Robert Carmack; *Guatemalan Rebellion: Unfinished History,* edited by Jonathan Fried; "Guatemala News in Brief," published by America's Watch and edited by Jean Marie Simon.

The poem Armando recites in Chapter I is Rainer Maria Rilke's "Archaic Torso of Apollo":

> We'll never know his legendary head
> whose eyes like ripening apples glowed.
> But even now his body glows like a lantern
> turned low, its flame restrained
>
> but burning. Without this flame the curve
> of his chest couldn't blind you, and the line
> of his thigh wouldn't gleam
> all the way to his potent center.
>
> Without this flame the stone would look less whole
> where it plunges from the shoulders,
> it wouldn't shine like the hide of a wild animal
>
> and light from every facet of this figure
> wouldn't burst like a shower of stars: for here
> no part fails to see you. You must change your life.

David Schweidel grew up in El Paso, Texas, three miles from the Mexican border. He remembers feeling like an anthropologist long before he knew what an anthropologist was. After studying anthropology at Stanford, UCLA, and the University of California, Berkeley, he received a Master of Fine Arts in creative writing from the University of Arizona and traveled to Central America, Mexico, the Caribbean, Europe, the South Pacific, North Africa, and the Middle East.

Schweidel's fiction and nonfiction have been published in several magazines, including *San Francisco Focus*, *East Bay Express*, *Kansas Quarterly*, *Cricket*, *Puerto del Sol*, and *Sonora Review*. Currently, he lives in Berkeley with his wife Linda and works at the University of California. His next book, a collaboration with author Robert Boswell, will be a nonfiction account of a New Mexico family's fifty-year search for the legendary treasure of Victorio Peak.

ACKNOWLEDGMENTS

The Vaclav Havel epigraph is from an interview with Erica Bain in the *London Times Literary Supplement*, January 23, 1987. Translated by A. G. Blain. Copyright © 1987 by Vaclav Havel. Used by permission.

The Gabriel Garcia Marquez epigraph is from his *The Autumn of the Patriarch*, translated by Gregory Rabassa (Harper and Row, 1976).

The Cesar Vallejo epigraph is from his poem "And what if after so many words," translated by Robert Bly with Douglas Lawder, published in *Neruda and Vallejo*, edited by Robert Bly (Beacon Press, 1971). Copyright © 1971 by Robert Bly. Used by permission from Robert Bly.

The Lawrence Durrell epigraph is from his *Balthazar* (E. P. Dutton and Co., 1958). Copyright © 1958 by Lawrence Durrell.

The George Orwell epigraph is from his *Burmese Days* (Harcourt, Brace, 1950). Copyright © 1934 by George Orwell.

The Thomas Gage epigraph is from *Travels in the New World*, edited by J. Eric S. Thompson (University of Oklahoma Press, 1958).

The John Lloyd Stevens epigraph is from *Incidents of Travel in Central America, Chiapas and Yucatan* (Dover Publications, 1969).

The three Antonio Machado epigraphs are from his "Campos de Castillo," published in *Manuel y Antonio Machado: Obras Completas* (Editorial Biblioteca Nueva, 1978). Copyright © 1978 by the heirs of Antonio Machado. Translations by David Schweidel.

The J. Geils epigraph is from the title of "Love Stinks" by The J. Geils Band.

The Pedro Calderon de la Barca epigraph is from his *La vida es sueno* (Espasa-Calpe, S. A., 1977).

The Julio Cortazar epigraph is from his short story "Blow-Up," published in *End of the Game and Other Stories*, translated by Paul Blackburn (Pantheon Books, 1967). Copyright © 1967, 1963 by Random House.

The C. P. Cavafy epigraph is from his poem "Che Fece . . . Il Gran Rifiuto," published in *Selected Poems*, translated by Edmund Keeley and Philip Sherrard (Princeton University Press, 1972). Copyright © 1972 by Edmund Keeley and Philip Sherrard. Used by permission from Princeton University Press.

The Theodore Roethke epigraph is from "Dolor," copyright © 1943 by Modern Poetry Association, Inc., from *The Collected Poems of Theodore Roethke* by Theodore Roethke. Used by permission of Doubleday, a division of Bantam Doubleday Dell Publishing Group.

Winners of the Milkweed National Fiction Prize:

Montana 1948
Larry Watson
(1993)

Larabi's Ox
Tony Ardizzone
(1992)

Aquaboogie
Susan Straight
(1990)

Blue Taxis
Eileen Drew
(1989)

Ganado Red
Susan Lowell
(1988)